The Early Middle Ages

Titles in the World History Series

**WORLD
HISTORY SERIES** ■ ■ ■

The Early
Middle Ages

by
James A. Corrick

Lucent Books, P.O. Box 289011, San Diego, CA 92198-9011

To Henry,
Who always comes through.

Library of Congress Cataloging-in-Publication Data

Corrick, James A.
    The early middle ages / by James A. Corrick.
       p. cm.—(World history series)
    Includes bibliographical references (p.) and index.
    ISBN 1-56006-246-0 (alk. paper)
    1. Europe—History—476-1492.   I. Title. II. Series.
D121.C67   1995
940.1—dc20   94-8778
                                           CIP
                                           AC

Copyright 1995 by Lucent Books, Inc., P.O. Box 289011,
San Diego, California, 92198-9011

Printed in the U.S.A.

Contents

Foreword

Each year on the first day of school, nearly every history teacher faces the task of explaining why his or her students should study history. One logical answer to this question is that exploring what happened in our past explains how the things we often take for granted—our customs, ideas, and institutions—came to be. As statesman and historian Winston Churchill put it, "Every nation or group of nations has its own tale to tell. Knowledge of the trials and struggles is necessary to all who would comprehend the problems, perils, challenges, and opportunities which confront us today." Thus, a study of history puts modern ideas and institutions in perspective. For example, though the founders of the United States were talented and creative thinkers, they clearly did not invent the concept of democracy. Instead, they adapted some democratic ideas that had originated in ancient Greece and with which the Romans, the British, and others had experimented. An exploration of these cultures, then, reveals their very real connection to us through institutions that continue to shape our daily lives.

Another reason often given for studying history is the idea that lessons exist in the past from which contemporary societies can benefit and learn. This idea, although controversial, has always been an intriguing one for historians. Those who agree that society can benefit from the past often quote philosopher George Santayana's famous statement, "Those who cannot remember the past are condemned to repeat it." Historians who ascribe to Santayana's philosophy believe that, for example, studying the events that led up to the major world wars or other significant historical events would allow society to chart a different and more favorable course in the future.

Just as difficult as convincing students to realize the importance of studying history is the search for useful and interesting supplementary materials that present historical events in a context that can be easily understood. The volumes in Lucent Books' World History Series attempt to present a broad, balanced, and penetrating view of the march of history. Ancient Egypt's important wars and rulers, for example, are presented against the rich and colorful backdrop of Egyptian religious, social, and cultural developments. The series engages the reader by enhancing historical events with these cultural contexts. For example, in *Ancient Greece*, the text covers the role of women in that society. Slavery is discussed in *The Roman Empire*, as well as how slaves earned their freedom. The numerous and varied aspects of everyday life in these and other societies are explored in each volume of the series. Additionally, the series covers the major political, cultural, and philosophical ideas as the torch of civilization is passed from ancient Mesopotamia and Egypt, through Greece, Rome, Medieval Europe, and other world cultures, to the modern day.

The material in the series is formatted in a thorough, precise, and organized manner. Each volume offers the reader a comprehensive and clearly written overview of an important historical event or period. The topic under discussion is placed in a broad, historical context. For example, *The Italian Renaissance* begins with a discussion of the High Middle Ages and the loss of central control that allowed certain Italian cities to develop artistically. The book ends by looking forward to the Reformation and interpreting the societal changes that grew out of the Renaissance. Thus, students are not only involved in an historical era, but also enveloped by the events leading up to that era and the events following it.

One important and unique feature in the World History Series is the primary and secondary source quotations that richly supplement each volume. These quotes are useful in a number of ways. First, they allow students access to sources they would not normally be exposed to because of the difficulty and obscurity of the original source. The quotations range from interesting anecdotes to far-sighted cultural perspectives and are drawn from historical witnesses both past and present. Second, the quotes demonstrate how and where historians themselves derive their information on the past as they strive to reach a consensus on historical events. Lastly, all of the quotes are footnoted, familiarizing students with the citation process and allowing them to verify quotes and/or look up the original source if the quote piques their interest.

Finally, the books in the World History Series provide a detailed launching point for further research. Each book contains a bibliography specifically geared toward student research. A second, annotated bibliography introduces students to all the sources the author consulted when compiling the book. A chronology of important dates gives students an overview, at a glance, of the topic covered. Where applicable, a glossary of terms is included.

In short, the series is designed not only to acquaint readers with the basics of history, but also to make them aware that their lives are a part of an ongoing human saga. Perhaps they will then come to the same realization as famed historian Arnold Toynbee. In his monumental work, *A Study of History*, he wrote about becoming aware of history flowing through him in a mighty current, and of his own life "welling like a wave in the flow of this vast tide."

Important Dates in the Early Middle Ages

378	400	450	500	550	600	650

A.D.

378
The Visigoths defeat a Roman army at Adrianople.

410-419
The Visigoths sack Rome; establish a kingdom in southern Gaul.

450
The Angles, Saxons, and Jutes invade Britain.

452
Attila and the Huns invade Italy but turn back before reaching Rome.

466
The Visigoths begin their conquest of Spain.

475
Theodoric becomes king of the Ostrogoths.

476
The western Roman Empire ends.

481
Under Clovis, who became the first Merovingian king, the Franks begin the conquest of Gaul.

493
Theodoric becomes the ruler of an Ostrogothic kingdom in Italy.

527
Justinian I becomes emperor of the Byzantine Empire.

532
The Nika revolt erupts in Constantinople.

535
The Byzantine Empire invades the Ostrogothic kingdom in Italy.

537
The Church of Santa Sophia in Constantinople is completed.

552
The Ostrogothic kingdom in Italy is destroyed.

554
The Byzantine Empire reaches its largest extent.

570
Muhammad is born in Mecca.

572
The Lombard kingdom is founded in northern Italy.

590
Gregory I becomes pope.

596
The conversion of England to Christianity is begun by missionaries sent by Pope Gregory I.

610
Heraclius becomes Byzantine emperor.

625
The Visigothic kingdom in Spain reaches its peak.

629
Heraclius defeats the Persians and recovers lost Byzantine territory.

630
Muhammad takes Mecca.

634
Muslim armies begin their conquest of the Near East.

639
The Muslims take Jerusalem.

679
The Bulgars enter the Balkans.

698
The Muslims conquer North Africa.

714
The Muslims conquer Spain.

717
The Muslims are unable to take Constantinople.

732
At the Battle of Tours, Charles Martel, Carolingian king, stops a Muslim advance into the kingdom of the Franks.

751
Pépin the Short becomes the Carolingian king of the Franks.

700	750	800	850	900	950	992

754
The Donation of Pépin helps create the Papal States.

771-772
Charlemagne becomes sole king of the Franks; begins his war against the Saxons.

778
Basques defeat Charlemagne's rear guard at Roncesvalles.

780
The Carolingian renaissance begins.

787
The Vikings begin raiding Britain.

800
Charlemagne is crowned emperor of the western Roman Empire.

811
The Bulgars defeat an invading Byzantine army and kill Emperor Nicephorus I.

827
The Muslims invade Sicily.

837
The Muslims invade Italy.

841
The Vikings begin raiding the Franks.

843
The Treaty of Verdun divides the Frankish empire among Charlemagne's grandsons and creates Carolingian kingdoms that will eventually become France and Germany.

846
The Muslims attack Rome.

867
Basil I becomes the first Macedonian emperor of the Byzantine Empire.

871
Alfred the Great becomes king of Wessex in Britain.

878
Alfred the Great defeats a Danish army that leads to establishment of the Danelaw in Britain.

885
The Vikings lay siege to Paris.

907
The Viking Oleg attacks Constantinople.

911
The Viking Rollo becomes the first duke of Normandy; Louis the Child, the last Carolingian king of the eastern Franks, dies.

916
The Muslims are driven out of Italy but remain in Sicily.

924
Berengar I, the last Carolingian emperor, is murdered.

936
Otto I becomes king of the eastern Franks.

962
Otto I becomes emperor of what was to be called the Holy Roman Empire.

985
The Vikings reach Greenland.

987
Louis V, king of the western Franks and the last Carolingian ruler, dies; Hugh Capet takes the throne.

992
The Viking Leif Ericsson reaches Vinland (North American coast).

A Crucial Time

To fifth-century Romans, "Europe was a backward, colonial region, receiving its . . . ideas from more advanced communities to the south and east."[1] Much of Europe— all of it north of the Danube River and east of the Rhine River—was wilderness inhabited by scattered tribes of German barbarians. A thousand years later, however, the wilderness was gone forever, and the German tribes had grown into nations, such as England and France, and had created their own civilizations whose ideas would spread over the entire planet. The thousand-year period that saw this change was the Middle Ages.

Feudalism and Chivalry

The Middle Ages started about A.D. 500, when the Roman Empire fell, and lasted until approximately A.D. 1500, when the Renaissance began. This period is also known as the Age of Feudalism and the Age of Chivalry because feudalism was the economic and political system under which much of Europe, particularly the western part, lived during this period. Chivalry was the code by which armored and mounted warriors, or knights, supposedly conducted themselves both on and off the battlefield.

The term *Middle Ages* was coined by the Italian historian Flavio Biondo in the fifteenth century. To Biondo and other Renaissance historians, the Middle Ages, or medieval period, was literally a middle period in the history of the world because it was sandwiched in between the classical period of Greek and Roman civilization and the Renaissance. Although present-day historians still call the fifth through the fifteenth centuries the Middle Ages, they now recognize that this thousand years was not a middle period in either the history of the world or even of Europe. To most modern scholars the Middle Ages is just another episode in the development of Western civilization from Greece to the present.

Renaissance historians, however, have had a longer-lasting effect on the general attitude toward the Middle Ages. These scholars depicted the Middle Ages as a backward time, in which people were ignorant and superstitious; art, literature, and learning disappeared; and progress of all sorts stopped. These historians believed that Renaissance Europe was the direct heir of ancient Greece and Rome and owed nothing to the ten centuries between the fall of Rome and their own time. The Middle Ages was nothing but a "thousand years of intellectual backwardness and social injustice separating classical antiquity from the enlightened modern age," according to David Nicholas.[2]

Nor is this view dead today. As historian Joseph R. Strayer points out:

> Many people still think . . . that the Middle Ages are merely a stagnant pit which lies between the heights of classical and of Renaissance civilization, and that all our legacy from the past was carried over the bridges which Renaissance thinkers threw across the medieval pit to the firm ground of Graeco-Roman learning.[3]

It is true that ignorance and superstition did exist during the Middle Ages. However, they also existed in ancient Greece and Rome and still exist today, and the extent of these and other problems of medieval society should not be exaggerated.

In reality the Middle Ages was no more backward than the classical world of Greece and Rome that came before it. True, its culture was different from those ancient ones, even though that culture grew out of those older societies, but its civilization was not inferior to that of the ancient world. Indeed, one reason that the Middle Ages is important to us is that it did create a civilization, as Strayer points out:

> It is because the history of the Middle Ages is the history of a civilization that the subject is worth studying . . . for the basic problems of all civilizations are similar. When we . . . understand how peoples of the past . . . accomplished their great . . . work . . . , then we will understand more about our own civilization.[4]

Additionally, the civilization of the Middle Ages is the direct ancestor of our

The Middle Ages became known as the Age of Chivalry. Chivalry was the code of ethics by which knights conducted their lives.

modern Western culture. The Middle Ages was an "epoch [time period] when forms and customs were in the making."[5] The French historian M. Paul Viollet says:

> We issue from [come out of] the Middle Ages. . . . The roots of our modern society lie deep in them. . . . What we are, we are in large measure because of the Middle Ages. The Middle Ages live in us; they are alive all around us.[6]

Many of the things that we now take for granted had their beginnings in the Middle Ages. Although ancient Greece and Rome were important to the development of the modern world, the Middle Ages gave us, for example, the concept of the nation. Before the Middle Ages, no such thing as a nation existed. Whereas in the twentieth century, the nation is the major political division, in the ancient world it was the city or city-state. Even the Roman Empire was a collection of cities, not nations. In learning about the beginnings of the nation and of nationalism in the Middle Ages, we learn much about the political struggles of the Western world from the Renaissance on.

And the nation is only one part of the modern world that comes from the Middle Ages. That period also produced representative government, capitalism, universities, experimental science, the Catholic and Orthodox Churches, romantic love, and modern towns and cities.

As with history in general, historians divide the Middle Ages into periods. The two major divisions are the Early, or Low, Middle Ages, from 500 to 1000, and the Late, or High, Middle Ages, from 1000 to 1500. The Early Middle Ages is also known as the Dark Ages because of the social chaos that followed the fall of Rome and because of the rapid loss of much Greek and Roman culture.

The Early Middle Ages is historically important for two reasons. First, it gave rise to the Late Middle Ages and, although, as Strayer says, "there are important differences between the early and late Middle Ages . . . these differences represent different stages in the development of a single civilization."[7] But more importantly, as Archibald R. Lewis observes:

A study of the early Middle Ages in Europe helps us to understand our own Western culture. . . . The early Middle

Ages . . . were the seedbed [source of development] out of which our modern Western world emerged; to understand them is to grasp the richness of our own special heritage.[8]

True, the people of the Early Middle Ages did lose a great deal of Roman civilization, although by no means all. However, in their attempt to rebuild that lost Roman culture, these citizens of the Early Middle Ages created entirely new ways of doing things. For example, feudalism was born. This political setup, which would reach its peak in the Late Middle Ages, worked by having one noble promise service, particularly military, to another noble in exchange for certain rights, such as the use of large estates.

Also during this period, new farm inventions produced more food more effi-

An illustration depicts the idealized orderliness of medieval society. The manor house of the lord sits in the background while peasants work the well-tended fields.

ciently. One of the most important of these inventions was a new kind of horse collar that allowed a horse to pull a plow. Thus, the new collar let horses plow more land than in premedieval times, resulting in larger harvests. The increased food production, in turn, paved the way for the population explosion of the Late Middle Ages, as well as of the Renaissance.

And it was the Early Middle Ages that moved European Civilization away from the Mediterranean Sea. Until A.D. 500, European civilization meant Mediterranean civilization because Europe's first two civilizations, Greek and Roman, were located on that great inland sea. However, when the Roman Empire fell apart, a shift began that moved European civilization north and west.

"Adjustment and Beginnings"

This shift partially resulted from the peoples of Europe trying to cope with the loss of the Roman Empire. Thus, the Early Middle Ages was "essentially a time of adjustment and beginnings," according to author Justine Davis Randers-Pehrson.[9]

The survivors of the fall of Rome lived in a Europe partially made up of the broken remains of the former empire. Towns, villages, and even whole regions that had been linked for centuries found themselves on their own. Used to being part of a whole that gave them their laws and their culture, people at first tried to cling to the old. What they could not hold on to they tried to rediscover.

The shift of European civilization north and west was also caused by the rise in the power of German barbarians. These Germans had been held in check by the Roman Empire until the beginning of the fifth century A.D. Then they overran the crumbling remains of the empire, taking control of it and the rest of western and northern Europe. During the centuries of the Early Middle Ages, the Germans would weld their culture to the remains of Greek and Roman civilization, producing, as historian Norman F. Cantor observes, an "era in which a distinctive western civilization emerged out of the background, one might almost say the clash, of Christian, Graeco-Roman, and Germanic institutions and ideas."[10] The new Europe of the Early Middle Ages would reach its full flowering in the Late Middle Ages of the eleventh through fifteenth centuries.

1 The Barbarian Invasions and the Fall of Rome

The Early Middle Ages had no clear-cut beginning, and "although change was rapid in the fifth century [A.D.], nowhere did a sharp break occur." The fall of Rome, which marked the end of the ancient world and the start of the medieval, was not a single event but a whole series as "the Roman Empire . . . evolved gradually into the Europe of the Germanic . . . kingdoms."[11]

Even after the empire was long gone, "men still gave their allegiance to its shadow," according to historian F.W. Walbank.[12]

Still, by tradition the date A.D. 476 has been used to mark the end of the Roman Empire and the beginning of the Middle Ages. In this year the emperor Romulus Augustulus (little Augustus) was deposed, and the first in a series of non-Roman

The beginning of the Middle Ages is traditionally A.D. 476, the year that Romulus Augustulus (pictured) was deposed and the first non-Roman kings took over the ruling of the empire.

kings took his place. With Romulus Augustulus's removal, Romans lost control of their own empire.

However, this imperial collapse affected only the western half of the Roman Empire. The eastern part, under its own emperor and called the Byzantine Empire, lasted another thousand years, becoming a major medieval power.

The Germans

Even before 476, the western Roman Empire had lost territory to invading German barbarians, who had captured and set up kingdoms in former Roman lands. The rulers of these kingdoms wanted nothing more than to rebuild the very empire that they helped smash. However, they would fail in that effort, and many of their own kingdoms would be swallowed up by other conquerors in the first few centuries of the Early Middle Ages.

The Romans called the Germans barbarians because they considered anyone who did not speak Latin or Greek to be a barbarian, even such people as the Egyptians. However, unlike the Egyptians the Germans were not civilized; that is, they did not have cities.

The Romans called all these northern barbarians *Germani*, even though that was actually the name for only one of the tribes. *Allemanni*, the name of another tribe, later became the word for "German" in French and Spanish. The Germans as a whole called themselves the *Theut*, which means "the people" and eventually gave us the word *Teuton*, or "German."

Until the first century A.D. the Germans were a collection of tribes living in what is now Denmark, northern Poland, and northern Germany. They lived in small villages, often with the houses built around a central point from which extended fields of barley, wheat, oats, and rye.

The tribes were actually groups of extended families, or clans, each claiming descent from a common ancestor. At the top of German society was the warrior, whose rank was determined either by that of his father or by that which he himself earned in battle. Such rank could be lost if a warrior were found doing manual labor, such as plowing a field or building a house. These jobs were considered lowly and were supposed to be done by women, children, slaves, and men unable to fight.

Few German clans were headed by a single chief. Instead, most practiced a rough form of democracy. A council made up of the senior men from each family made day-to-day decisions, but anything important had to be voted on by all the clan's warriors. The Roman historian Tacitus described such clan meetings in his *Germania*:

> Concerning minor matters the chiefs deliberate, but in important affairs all the . . . [warriors] are consulted, although the subjects referred to the common people for judgment are discussed beforehand by the chiefs. Unless some sudden and unexpected event calls them together they assemble on fixed days. . . . They do not reckon time by the number of days . . . but by the number of nights. . . . When the crowd is sufficient they take their place fully armed. Silence is proclaimed by the priests, who have . . . the right to keep order. Then the king or a chief addresses [the assembled

The Germans were pagans who worshiped a number of gods. The main German god was one-eyed Odin.

their gods would be killed in a final battle with giants and other evil forces.

The chief German god and father of humankind was the one-eyed Odin. Other major gods were Thor, Tiu (also known as Tyr or Tiwaz), and Woden, all of whom were gods of war. These war gods were a demanding lot, and bands of German warriors often sacrificed both loot and prisoners to them. The Germans also had goddesses of the harvest, Nerthus, and of love, Freya. Several of the days of the week are named for these German gods: Tuesday is Tiu's day; Wednesday, Woden's day; Thursday, Thor's; and Friday, Freya's.

Contact Between Rome and the Germans

In the first century A.D. a growing population forced some German clans to migrate south, where they hoped to find more room. They quickly ran up against the northern borders of the Roman Empire, marked by the Rhine and Danube Rivers. They were generally unsuccessful in forcing their way across these rivers and into the empire itself, although two tribes, the Cimbri and the Teutones, cut their way across Gaul (present-day France) and into Italy, where they were defeated by the Romans in A.D. 102.

The Germans at this time were no match for the better-armed and trained Roman soldiers. Although these first-century Germans had iron weapons, their iron was generally not of good quality. Tacitus observed: "Iron is [not] abundant. . . . Some few use iron weapons or long spears [made all of iron], but usually they carry

warriors]. . . . If an opinion is displeasing they reject it by shouting; if they agree to it they clash with their spears.[13]

The Germans were pagans or non-Christians, who had a number of gods. Like the gods of the ancient Greeks and the Romans, the German gods were a very human bunch, who could be jealous, envious, and sometimes even downright petty. However, unlike the Greeks and Romans, the northern barbarians believed that javelins . . . tipped with a short narrow piece of iron."[14]

Although the Germans could not force their way into the empire, they found they could enter it as single individuals and small family groups. So, many of them drifted across the borders, becoming farm workers and soldiers. German and Roman traders also crossed the border, particularly as the northern barbarians learned the value of Roman goods. Thus, by the year 400, the line dividing the German and Roman worlds was no longer sharp. Germans were scattered throughout the empire, and the western Roman army was made up mostly of German officers and men.

A Barbarian Victory at Adrianople

In A.D. 378 the Visigoths defeated an eastern Roman army at Adrianople. The victory showed the Germans that the Romans could no longer protect their lands and paved the way for the founding of the German kingdoms of the Early Middle Ages. The Roman soldier Ammianus Marcellinus fought at Adrianople and later described the battle in his Roman History, *as quoted in* A Source Book of Medieval History.

"After marching eight miles, our men came in sight of the wagons of the enemy, which . . . [were] arranged in a circle. According to their custom, the barbarian host [army] raised a fierce and hideous yell, while the Roman generals marshalled [arranged] their line of battle . . . .

And while arms and missiles of all kinds were meeting in fierce conflict, . . . our men began to retreat; but presently . . . they made a fresh stand, and the battle increased . . . terrifying our soldiers, numbers of whom were pierced by strokes of the javelins hurled at them, and by arrows.

Then the two lines of battle dashed against each other. . . . Our left wing had advanced . . . but they were deserted by the rest of the cavalry, and . . . beaten down. . . . Presently, our infantry also was left unsupported. . . . And by this time such clouds of dust arose that it was scarcely possible to see the sky, which resounded with terrible cries. . . . The barbarians . . . beat down our horses and men and left no spot to which our ranks could fall back to operate. . . .

Amid all this great . . . confusion our infantry were exhausted by toil and danger, until at last they had neither the strength left to fight nor spirit to plan anything. . . . The sun . . . scorched the Romans. . . . At last our columns were entirely beaten back. . . .

Scarcely one third of the whole army escaped."

Once the Roman Empire weakened, the German tribes succeeded in invading Italy. Here, German tribes pass from Italy into Gaul.

The Visigoths

For almost three hundred years the Romans kept the Germans from successfully invading the empire. However, in the fifth century the borders fell, and barbarian armies marched into the empire and often into Italy. These invasions succeeded because the empire was no longer able to defend itself and because Germans who had traded and soldiered in the empire spread detailed reports about imperial weaknesses to the clans outside the empire.

The first important German invasion was that of the Visigoths who, in 410, captured Rome. In the second century the Visigoths, or West Goths, had settled in what would later become Romania. For the next two hundred years they farmed and hunted this land, as well as traded with the Roman Empire.

Around 376, the Visigoths were driven from their land by the Huns, a nomadic people who invaded Europe from the central plains of Asia. Having lost their homes, some sixty thousand men, women, and children pushed south across the Danube and into Roman lands. The Visigoths found themselves in the eastern half of the empire, and after defeating a Roman army and killing the eastern emperor, the Visigoths struck a deal with the western emperor, who allowed them to settle on land just south of the Danube. However, dissatisfaction with this agreement grew among the Germans, and led by the war chieftain Alaric, bands of Visigoths began raiding northern Italy in 402.

Finally, in 409, Alaric and his army managed to drive deep into Italy. The invading barbarians marched quickly to Rome, where they spent three days looting before continuing south.

Alaric died soon after the taking of Rome, and the Visigoths once more turned north, this time invading Gaul. The Roman authorities worked out another deal with them that gave the Germans the Aquitaine region in southern Gaul as a separate Gothic kingdom. The Visigoths would eventually push their kingdom farther south into Spain.

The Visigothic kingdom was only the first of many Early Middle Ages kingdoms, for as Crane Brinton and his coauthors note in *A History of Civilization*:

The Visigoths were pioneers, signs of what was to come. They gained the first spectacular field victories over the Romans, and their kingdom . . . was the precedent [model] for a whole . . . series of barbarian "concessions" within the Empire.[15]

These concessions meant that Rome lost control of large sections of its western empire. Thus, to the Visigoths, the western Romans gave up southern Gaul and, eventually, all of Spain. Other concessions would take more land away from the western empire, until little was left but Italy. Over the next few centuries many of these concessions would form the kingdoms of the Middle Ages, eventually becoming modern European nations.

In 409, the war chieftain Alaric (pictured above, and below on horse) led his bands to a final conquest of Rome. Although Roman authorities tried to appease the German barbarians, the Germans were not satisfied until they had conquered Roman territory.

Choosing to Live Among the Barbarians

While the Germans generally admired the Roman Empire, most imperial citizens disliked the barbarians' way of life. However, fifth-century Roman trader Priscus in An Embassy to the Huns, *quoted in* Medieval Europe: A Short Sourcebook, *described a Roman who was living among a group of barbarians, the Scythians, because he preferred these people to the Romans.*

"[The former Roman citizen] considered his new life among the Scythians better than his old life among the Romans, and the reasons he urged were as follows: 'After war the Scythians live at leisure, enjoying what they have got, and not at all, or very little, disturbed. The Romans, on the other hand, are in the first place very liable to be killed, if there are any hostilities, since they have to rest their hopes of protection on others, and are not allowed, by their tyrants, to use arms. And . . . [professional soldiers] who do use them [weapons] are injured by the cowardice of their generals, who cannot properly conduct war.

'But the condition of Roman subjects in time of peace is far more grievous [painful] than the evils of war, for the exaction of [taking of] . . . taxes is very severe, and unprincipled men inflict injuries on others because the laws are . . . not valid against all classes [of society]. A transgressor [nontaxpayer] who belongs to the wealthy classes is not punished for his injustice, while a poor man, who does not understand business, undergoes the legal penalty . . . . The climax of misery is to have to pay in order to obtain justice. For no one will give a hearing to the injured man except he pay . . . money to the judge and the judge's clerks.'"

The Vandals

In addition to the land they took from the Roman west, the Visigoths also allowed other invaders to move into the western empire. Constant Visigothic attacks forced the Romans to pull troops away from the Rhine and Danube borders and out of Britain altogether. So, while Alaric and his Goths marched into Italy, other Germans, among them the Vandals, charged across the Rhine and looted and burned their way down through Gaul and Spain. Some of these barbarians grabbed imperial land and held on to it. The Vandals, however, continued on into North Africa, eventually establishing a short-lived kingdom in Carthage in 439, the ancient city and former enemy of Rome.

In 455 the Vandals launched their own attack against the city of Rome, which they

The Vandals invaded and conquered European cities in efficient, brutal attacks. In 455 they launched their own attack on Rome, and after a naval battle, successfully conquered and looted the city.

took after a naval battle. *Vandal* has come down to us as a word for someone who destroys things for the sheer fun of it. Yet the Vandals were no more destructive than the Visigoths, and after having looted Rome, they returned to their North African homes, where they were soon assimilated into the native population and disappeared from the stage of history.

Attila and the Huns

Not all the invaders of the Roman Empire were German, and the most feared of these non-Germans were the Huns, the Asian nomads who drove the Visigoths into the empire. These nomads were a serious threat to both the remains of the empire and the new German kingdoms. In the late fifth century under their leader Attila, the Huns seemed ready to conquer all of eastern and western Europe.

By the beginning of the fifth century, the Huns had carved out an empire that stretched from the Caspian Sea to the Alps, an area almost as large as the entire Roman Empire, although with far fewer people and far less wealth. These nomads were excellent horsemen and inspired fear because of their ferocious charges and unpredictable but winning battle tactics. To many of their enemies they seemed almost supernatural, as their mounted archers hit targets with amazing accuracy.

In 434 Attila and his brother became co-kings of the Huns, although within a few years, Attila killed his brother and became the sole ruler of the nomads. According to the sixth-century Gothic historian Jordanes, Attila was an imposing figure:

> [Attila] was a man born into the world to shake the nations, the scourge [cause of great affliction] of all lands, who in some way terrified all mankind by the rumors . . . concerning him. He was haughty in his walk . . . so that the power of his proud spirit appeared in the movement of his body. He was indeed a lover of war, yet restrained in action; mighty in counsel [giving advice] . . . lenient to those who were received under his protection.[16]

In 451, after a series of successful campaigns against the eastern empire that brought the Huns much gold and other

Attila and the Huns were such powerful and skilled soldiers that many of their enemies thought they possessed supernatural powers. While the Huns plundered Italy, Rome was spared because the Huns feared the plague that was then ravaging the city.

loot, Attila turned his attention to the western empire because it seemed to him an easier target than the eastern. However, the west proved to be stronger than it appeared. Invading Gaul, Attila suffered his only defeat, being beaten by a combined Roman and Visigoth army.

Refusing to give up, the Hun leader quickly regrouped and sent his army swarming into Italy. Although the Huns

looted several cities, they left Rome alone. Tradition has it that Pope Leo the Great (Leo I) talked Attila out of plundering the western empire's capital, but in reality, it was the plague and famine sweeping Italy at the time of the invasion that saved Rome. Afraid of the disease and unable to feed themselves in the famine-gripped land, the Huns had to turn and retreat before they reached Rome.

Not long after this retreat, Attila died. The Hun empire was then divided among his many sons, who quarreled and fought among themselves over its parts. Various conquered peoples, seeing their chance, revolted, thus ending the Hun empire and their threat to both the old Roman Empire and the new German kingdoms.

The Ostrogoths

The Visigoths, the Vandals, and the Huns swept through Italy, taking and looting cities and then leaving. But the next set of invaders, the Ostrogoths, came and stayed. Indeed, these new invaders tried to remake the remains of the western empire into something like its old self.

The Ostrogoths, or East Goths, were from the same region as the Visigoths, but they had lived farther east and thus had been conquered by the Huns. In the late fifth century they broke away from Hun rule and moved west toward the Roman Empire.

In the years since the Visigoths, Vandals, and Huns, important changes had taken place in the western empire. First, the capital was no longer Rome, but Ravenna, a Roman naval port located on the Adriatic Sea not far from Venice. The imperial government had moved to Ravenna because of the repeated lootings of Rome. The new capital, although it sat in the middle of a swamp, was more easily defended.

Second, a non-Roman, the barbarian Odoacer, was now ruler. Although the barbarian had deposed the last western Roman emperor, he had not tried to become emperor himself. Instead, with the permission of the eastern emperor, who saw himself now as sole emperor of both the western and eastern empires, Odoacer ruled as a viceroy, or imperial representative, over the west.

Under Odoacer, life in the western empire continued much as it had. However, the barbarian viceroy became more and more powerful and independent of eastern control, and Zeno, then emperor of the eastern empire, decided that Odoacer had to go.

In 488 Zeno invited the Ostrogoths to invade Italy and to take Ravenna from Odoacer. The eastern emperor thought this a good plan because it would take care of Odoacer and also get rid of the Ostrogoths, who had been steadily raiding across the eastern imperial border for some years.

Under the leadership of the chieftain Theodoric, the Ostrogoths captured the western capital and killed Odoacer. For a time Theodoric kept his relations with the eastern empire friendly, but these relations became strained as Theodoric operated as though the remains of the western empire were an Ostrogothic kingdom and he were king. And, indeed, for all practical purposes, the Ostrogoth was king of a German kingdom in Italy. Still, he never declared himself as such and thus never officially broke away from the eastern empire.

Like Odoacer, the Ostrogoth, now known as Theodoric the Great, kept the western empire Roman. Theodoric even tried to reform the imperial government by putting a stop to the widespread corruption of the Roman civil service and by lowering taxes. He launched an ambitious program that cleaned up harbors, repaired aqueducts, and restored churches and public buildings.

Like most Germans, Theodoric admired the old empire and its accomplishments. His feelings about the empire and about his duties are clear in a public letter he issued, as quoted by Brian Tierney:

While other barbarian tribes had merely looted Rome and moved on, the Ostrogoths, led by Theodoric (here entering Rome), held onto Rome and tried to restore its former greatness.

The Ostrogoths kill the non-Roman emperor Odoacer. The Ostrogoths invaded the western empire at the invitation of Zeno, emperor of the eastern empire, who believed Odoacer had become too powerful and independent.

We [Theodoric] delight to live after the law of the Romans, whom we seek to defend . . . and we are as much interested in the maintenance of morality as we can possibly be in war. For what profit is there in having removed the turmoil of the Barbarians unless we live according to law? . . . Let other kings desire the glory of battles won, of cities taken, of ruins made; our purpose is . . . so to rule that our subjects shall grieve that they did not earlier acquire the blessing of our dominion [rule].[17]

Many of Theodoric's subjects did come to appreciate his rule. According to the Byzantine scholar Procopius:

Theodoric was exceedingly careful to observe justice . . . and attained the highest degree of wisdom. . . . Although in name he was a usurper [one who seizes illegally], yet in fact he was as truly an emperor as any who have distinguished themselves in this office from the beginning of time. Both the Goths and Romans loved him greatly. . . . When he died he had not only made himself an object of terror to his enemies, but he also left to his subjects a keen sense of bereavement and loss.[18]

Like Procopius, Theodoric saw himself as a Roman ruler. However, the Ostro-

The Rule of Theodoric the Great

The following extracts from the letters of Cassiodorus, Theodoric the Great's secretary, as quoted in Brian Tierney's The Middle Ages, *illustrate the Ostrogothic ruler's intense interest in the welfare of the people he governed. They also show that Theodoric was no fool and wanted a strict accounting of all money spent on public projects.*

"We [Theodoric] hear with sorrow . . . that you the Fathers of the State [Roman Senate], who ought to set an example to your sons (the ordinary citizens), have been so remiss [careless] in the payment of taxes that on the first collection nothing, or next to nothing, has been brought in from any Senatorial house . . . . Now then, . . . pay the taxes . . . [for which] each one of you is liable. . . .

If the people of Rome will beautify their City we will help them. Institute a strict audit . . . of the money given by us to the different workmen for the beautification of the City. See that we are receiving money's worth for the money spent. . . .We expect the Romans to help from their own resources in this patriotic work, and certainly not to intercept our contributions for this purpose. . . .

Let nothing lie useless which may redound to [have a good effect on] the beauty of the City. . . . Cause the blocks of marble which are everywhere lying about in ruins to be wrought [constructed] into walls. . . . Only take care to use only those stones which have really fallen from public buildings, as we do not wish to appropriate private property, even for the glorification of the City. . . .

It should be only the surplus of the crops of any Province, beyond what is needed for the supply of its own wants, that should be exported. Station persons in the harbours to see that foreign ships do not take away produce to foreign shores until the Public Providers have got all that they require. . . .

Impress upon all . . . subordinates that we would rather that our Treasury lost a suit than that it gained one wrongfully, rather that we lost money than that the taxpayer was driven to suicide. . . .

We cannot command the religion of our subjects, since no-one can be forced to believe against his will."

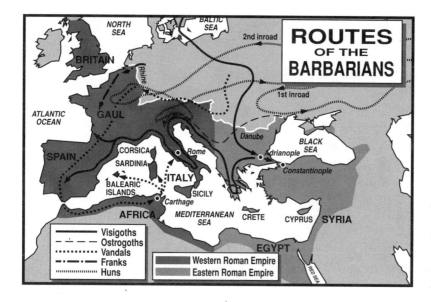

ROUTES OF THE BARBARIANS

Visigoths
Ostrogoths
Vandals
Franks
Huns

Western Roman Empire
Eastern Roman Empire

A map clearly shows the path of destruction followed by the various barbarian tribes as they looted their way through the remnants of the former Roman Empire.

goths as a whole remained outsiders. In part Theodoric encouraged this separation between the Goths and the Romans. He was afraid that if his German followers became civilized they would become soft and no longer make good warriors.

In part, however, the separation between Ostrogoths and Romans was a matter of religion. Although the Ostrogoths had converted to Christianity even before they escaped the Huns, they were not members of the Catholic Church as were the citizens of both halves of the Roman Empire. The Goths' brand of Christianity, Arianism, was somewhat different. Unlike the Romans, the Ostrogoths did not believe that God, Christ, and the Holy Ghost were equal parts of a single being, the Trinity. Instead, the Germans thought that God was superior to Christ because he had fathered Jesus, who was therefore neither completely divine nor completely human.

Such a difference in belief was very important to these early Christians, and it created more of a division between the Goths and the rest of the western empire than any other single thing. Indeed, toward the end of Theodoric's rule, it led several Roman nobles to plot against the Ostrogothic ruler. These Catholic Romans were afraid that anti-Catholic Germans were becoming too powerful in Theodoric's court. Upon discovering this plot, Theodoric had two of the nobles executed and began a general persecution of Catholic Christians in Italy.

The Final Crisis

Upon Theodoric's death in 526, his nine-year-old grandson became king. Since the boy was too young to govern, his mother Amalasuntha, who was Theodoric's daughter, was the actual ruler, or regent. Although intelligent, capable, and well educated, Amalasuntha was unable to win over the Gothic aristocracy, partially because they resented taking orders from a woman. The German nobles also disliked Amalasuntha's giving her son a Roman education rather than a Gothic one, which stressed war and fighting.

However, Amalasuntha managed to keep her power because it was her son, not herself, who was technically the ruler. She also strengthened her position by finding strong political allies, such as the emperor of the eastern empire. And, when all else failed, she had her enemies killed.

When Amalasuntha's son died at the age of sixteen, she found that the Goths would no longer follow her orders. She, therefore, asked her cousin, Theodahad, to become her coruler. The agreement was that, although Theodahad would have the title of king, Amalasuntha would be the actual ruler. As soon as Theodahad became king, he had Amalasuntha thrown into prison. Soon after, she was strangled by followers of some of her political enemies whom she had previously had killed.

In the eastern empire news of this murder was seen as the perfect excuse for retaking the west from the Goths. The eastern emperor Justinian I sent an army immediately to Italy to seek revenge for the killing of his ally, Amalasuntha, and to return the west to rule by members of the Catholic Church.

The east's invasion seemed to go well, and the eastern troops took Rome and then Ravenna. However, this first campaign merely sparked a long string of wars between the eastern empire's army and the Ostrogoths that raged up and down the Italian peninsula for the next several years until 552. In the end, the Goths were thrown out of Italy, leaving the eastern empire in control.

However, after almost twenty years of war, even the remains of the western Roman Empire were gone. Rome itself was wrecked more thoroughly by this war than by all the previous German raids combined. The remaining sections of the western empire had easily broken away from imperial control, and the eastern empire had no resources left to reconquer them. By the middle of the sixth century the western Roman Empire was shattered forever. The Early Middle Ages was fully underway.

The Legacy of Rome

The Roman Empire was gone but not forgotten, and the important thing that would be remembered through the next several centuries was that Rome had given order and provided culture to a huge territory. Although much of Rome's legacy was lost, the Germans, now scattered throughout what was to become western Europe, would seek to keep as much of that legacy as possible. As historian David Nicholas notes, "The civilization of medieval Europe was founded on the accomplishments of the Romans."[19]

In the west no organization saved more of that Roman legacy than the Christian church. Although far from being the powerful force it was to become in later centuries, it still greatly influenced the years and decades following the fall of Rome. Outside of the eastern Roman Empire, it alone still had a central authority whose agents were spread over all of western Europe. The church would not only provide the core around which the society of the Early Middle Ages would grow, but it would also give this period much of its substance and color.

Chapter

2 Upon This Rock: The Importance of the Christian Church

By the late sixth century no central political authority existed in western Europe, which was now a patchwork of different-sized German kingdoms. However, one or-

The tenets of the Christian church spread throughout Europe during the Middle Ages via missionaries. Gregory the Great sent Christian missionaries into England.

ganization had survived the breakup of the Roman Empire, the Christian church, which, as the Early Middle Ages began, continued the expansion that it had begun in the last centuries of the Roman Empire. The church's missionaries worked their way into northern Europe and converted the Germans to Christianity.

West and East

The church of Rome that survived the fall of the western empire and the church of the Byzantine Empire were supposedly two branches of the same organization. Both were part of the Catholic Church. However, the western church often acted independently of the eastern branch.

One difference between the two sections of the church was that, in the west, the head was the pope, and in the east, it was the Byzantine emperor. Both pope and emperor claimed that they were the spiritual leader of the whole church.

This and other differences caused a great deal of friction between the popes and the Byzantine emperors. During the Early Middle Ages the two branches of the church sometimes moved far apart, as in the eighth century, when they almost split from one another over the use of religious statues and painted images in churches. At other times, they drifted closer together, as in the seventh century, when faced with the spread of the new religion of Islam.

However, eventually the differences between the two became so great that they broke permanently from one another. The western church kept the name Catholic Church, while the eastern became the Orthodox Church, or Eastern Orthodox Church as they both are still known today.

The Western Church and Medieval Civilization

Even within the western church, differences existed among its officials and its members. Arguments raged, and continued to rage—even into the present—over the meaning of the Bible, over ritual, and even over church leadership. Thus, the church of Rome was not so unified in its views that it blanketed and then smothered all the individual features of the many societies that came into it, thereby creating a single medieval culture. Even in the Late Middle Ages, European medieval civilization varied from region to region, much as current Western culture varies from one part of the world to another.

Still, the western church did insist that its members hold certain beliefs that became part of the overall western medieval civilization. Certain church-promoted ideas began to appear in all of the Christian parts of western Europe. In addition to a belief in salvation, good church members felt that self-discipline, moderation, and self-denial were virtues, as were social responsibility and charity. They saw the world as a testing ground of their faith and believed that, even though this world was not perfect, it could be made better. They believed that God and his world could be approached through thought and study. Yet, they were also afraid that "the human mind . . . [could] *think away the supernatural*," according to historian Crane Brinton.[20]

It is because the medieval church spread these ideas throughout western Europe that some, such as self-discipline, moderation, and charity, became part of present-day Western culture. Both moderation and self-discipline were brought forward by the church from the classical Greeks and Romans. Charity, however, was not practiced in the ancient world, nor did it become important in Western culture until the Early Middle Ages and encouragement by the church.

The Western Church and Local Government

The western Christian church was able to expand and to become a major social and cultural force in the Early Middle Ages for a number of reasons. First, most of the clergy could read and write, which throughout the Early Middle Ages few people outside the church could do. This church monopoly resulted in priests' being in civil government, since only they had the skills needed to write letters and keep records. The word *clerical*, meaning "office work", comes from this medieval practice of using priests, or clerics, as secretaries.

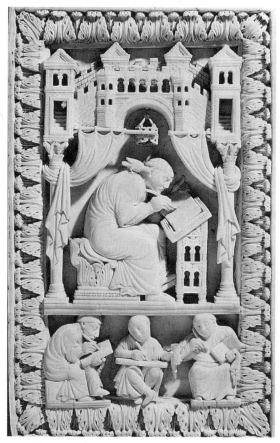

Because members of the clergy could write, the Christian church became a social and cultural force during the Middle Ages. Clerics' skills were needed in civil government, and thus government functions became mixed with Christian ideals.

High church officials were often part of nonchurch, or secular, government; for example, in the east, the Byzantine emperor Justinian I "had formerly confirmed the position of bishops as judge, financial officers, and legal protectors of their city," according to historians David Knowles and Dimitri Obolensky.[21] In some medieval cities, the church provided the only local government.

Since church officials could, and often did, take an active part in local politics, their promotion to higher positions within the church became more than mere church business, and local rulers often took a hand in the selection of archbishops and bishops. Thus, in 845, Hincmar became archbishop of Rheims because he was nominated and supported by the Frankish king Charles the Bald. Hincmar ran the local government and served as a political advisor to Charles, as well as seeing to church affairs.

In Germany during the last part of the Early Middle Ages, when a new bishop or archbishop was needed, the German king filled the position with the candidate he liked best, without consulting the church. The church, feeling it should have control over its own appointments, finally forced the German rulers to stop this practice in the first century of the Late Middle Ages. However, in the west, medieval secular rulers continued to fight with the church over who should appoint local church officials.

Out of this struggle between western secular and religious rulers would eventually come one of our major democratic principles, the guaranteed rights of the individual. Church and state put very real limits on each other's power by each's insistence that its rights be protected. As historian Crane Brinton observes, "This acceptance [of protected but limited rights] is . . . one of the roots of what we now call 'civil rights' of the individual and of smaller groups within the political state," because in the seventeenth and eighteenth centuries, western European philosophers decided that such protected rights also applied to individual people.[22] This idea of individual rights became one of the cornerstones of our modern democracy.

Missionary Work, Converts and Heretics

Another reason that the western church was so influential was that it converted many northern German tribes to Christianity. This conversion was done through active and aggressive missionary work, which gave the church of Rome a large, loyal following.

According to historian David Nicholas, the church's success among the Germans was due in part to the missionaries' ability to make use of the local culture:

> The missionaries were careful to emphasize the heroic deeds of Old Testament figures in preaching to the Germans. Jesus's power was emphasized, and his statement that he came to bring not peace but a sword was convenient. Jesus is . . . [represented as] a warrior on horseback in some Germanic sculptures.
>
> The spread of Christianity in the north . . . owed much to politics. . . . The Germans identified the ruler with the gods and his tribe, and Christian missionaries always converted the kings before preaching to their subjects. Since the king and in some cases the aristocracy possessed divine attributes as descendants of Wotan, the chief [German] god, the conversion of the rulers was all that was needed.[23]

The church also accepted some aspects of each local religion in order to encourage acceptance of Christianity. For example, it allowed some non-Christian holidays to continue, and it even adopted certain non-Christian customs, some of which are still in use today, such as having a tree and mistletoe at Christmas. However, the church never allowed its basic structure or beliefs to be changed. Nor did it accept other gods, such as Thor or Odin, because to do so would have meant giving up the central Christian idea of a single God.

Finally, the western church was able to defeat rival Christian groups whose beliefs, labeled heresies, often offered stiff competition for converts. By the end of the Early Middle Ages, the church's missionary work had stamped out such heresies as the Arianism of the Goths, and it became the only Christian organization of any importance in western Europe. It would not face any major Christian competition until the Protestant Reformation of the sixteenth century. However, from the seventh through the tenth centuries, it would be seriously tested by the eruption of Islam out of Arabia.

Western Church Structure

The basic hierarchy, or ruling body, of the western church was already established by the beginning of the Early Middle Ages. At the bottom of the clergy were the priests, then came the bishops, and finally, at the top, the pope.

Priests made up the largest part of the clergy, with each priest being in charge of a church. The word *priest* comes from the Greek word *presbyteros* (elder) from which, much later, the Protestant Presbyterian sect would take its name. Priests received formal training before being appointed by higher church officials to specific areas.

The running of the church fell mostly to priests who had been promoted to

A Missionary to Medieval Britain

In The Ecclesiastical [Religious] History of the English People, *excerpted from* A Source Book of Medieval History, *the eighth-century Benedictine monk Bede tells how missionaries, headed by the monk Augustine, converted the southern Saxons, one of the German tribes who had conquered Britain in the previous century. Such active export of Christianity helped the western church gain its hold over so much of Europe during the Middle Ages. As was standard practice, the missionaries converted the local king first.*

"[The missionaries] . . . were on their journey seized with a sudden fear and began to think of returning home, rather than of proceeding to a barbarous, fierce, and unbelieving nation, to whose very languages they were strangers . . . . The Pope [Gregory I] . . . sent them an encouraging letter, persuading them to proceed in the work . . . and rely on the assistance of the Almighty. . . .

Augustine, thus strengthened . . . , arrived in Britain. The powerful Ethelbert was at that time king of Kent [region in southeast England]. . . . [The missionaries] had taken interpreters . . . and sending to Ethelbert, signified that they . . . brought a joyful message, which . . . assured . . . all who took advantage of it everlasting joys in a kingdom that would never end [heaven], with the living and true God. The king . . . had before heard of the Christian religion, having a Christian wife. . . .

When Augustine . . . had preached to [Ethelbert] . . . , the king answered thus: 'Your words . . . are very fair, but as they are new to us, and of uncertain import [meaning], I cannot . . . forsake that which I have so long followed. . . . But . . . we will not . . . forbid you to preach and win as many as you can to your religion.'. . .

As soon as [the missionaries] entered the dwelling place assigned them, they began . . . living . . . in conformity with what they prescribed for others. . . . There was . . . a church . . . built whilst the Romans were still in the island [Britain], . . . [in which] they first began to . . . preach, and to baptize, until the king being converted to the faith, allowed them to preach openly. . . .

When [Ethelbert] . . . was baptized, greater numbers began daily to . . . [abandon] their heathen rites. . . . Their conversion the king encouraged in so far that he compelled none to embrace Christianity, but only showed more affection to the believers."

bishops. The word *bishop* comes from the Greek word *episkopos* (overseer), which also gives us the word *episcopal* (relating to a bishop). Each bishop was supposedly a direct spiritual heir of Christ's, and each was in charge of a large area known as a bishopric or a see that contained several churches. Sometimes an archbishop was placed over several bishoprics.

The bishops formed a council that ran the church. Such councils decided which Christian writings were divinely inspired, who were the true prophets, and which religious practices should be accepted.

The Bishop of Rome

The most important bishop in the western church was that of Rome, for he was the pope and claimed supreme authority over all the other bishops. In the west bishops generally accepted this claim and the authority of the pope. However, eastern bishops rejected it. This rejection was another of the many issues that divided the eastern and western churches.

The pope's authority came in large part from his being located in Rome,

In this illustration based on an early medieval manuscript, the clergy marches in procession before the emperor. At times, many church officials, including popes, were chosen by noble families. When these church officials did not please the nobles, they were killed and replaced with more cooperative individuals.

which even long after the western empire collapsed was seen by western Europe as a center of power. Rome had also been the city from which most secular court decisions had come, so it was logical for the bishop of Rome to settle the tricky issues of Christianity.

At the beginning of the Early Middle Ages, however, the pope's actual power was limited because he had no way to enforce orders on clergy outside of Italy. But, as the Early Middle Ages wore on, the pope gained more real power when he, and not church councils, began selecting archbishops and bishops. These church officials chosen by the pope tended to be more loyal and more obedient to the pope than did those who had come to office independently of him.

Popes of the Early Middle Ages often found themselves at the mercy of secular groups. Thus, during the last part of the eighth century and the first part of the ninth, the Frankish king and emperor Charlemagne, not the pope, called church councils and made decisions about basic church policy. Charlemagne had gained this authority through the Franks' wars against the Lombards. He, and not the pope, wielded the real power in northern and central Italy.

During the Early Middle Ages the pope was not necessarily selected by church officials, election by the College of Cardinals not being established until the eleventh century. Instead, popes were often chosen by the noble families of Rome. This latter practice was very common in the ninth and tenth centuries, during which the papacy lost almost all the power that it had gained up to that time. A pope who fell out of favor with these noble families was killed by them and a new one elected.

Gregory the Great

The first strong pope in the Early Middle Ages was Gregory I, or Gregory the Great, who was one of the most important church officials of the period and who actively sought to reform and expand the church. Born of a noble Roman family, Gregory was prefect, or mayor, of Rome for a time and then, wanting a more spiritual life, founded seven monasteries. In 576 he entered the one that he established in Rome.

In 590 Gregory was elected pope. Unwilling at first to leave the monastery, he tried to refuse the position. However, once in office, he set out energetically to correct the problems he saw in the church. His reforms touched on everything from church ritual to the moral conduct of the clergy. For the latter, he insisted that priests not marry nor engage in sexual activity. This ban was in part to keep priests from handing church offices down to their children.

As pope, Gregory continued to dress in his coarse monk's robe and eat the cheapest of foods. Instead of using church money for new buildings, he spent it on charity. Historian Will Durant notes that Gregory ensured that every poor family in Rome had "a [monthly] portion of corn, wine, cheese, vegetables, oil, fish, meat, clothing, and money; and every day his agents brought cooked provisions to the sick."[24]

Gregory was also enthusiastic about education, but only as long as it was Christian learning. He did much to popularize Christian thought through his own writing, such as his biography of Saint Benedict; his *Dialogues*, which contained stories about holy

Gregory the Great Instructs His Priests and Bishops

In 590, just after becoming pope, Gregory the Great wrote The Book of the Pastoral Rule, *in which he explains how he expects priests and bishops to perform their duties. This work became the handbook for both bishops and priests during the Middle Ages. The excerpt that follows is from Frederick Ogg's* A Source Book of Medieval History.

"The ruler [the priest] should always be pure in thought . . . ; for the hand that would cleanse dirt must needs be clean, lest . . . it soil all the more whatever it touches.

The ruler should always be a leader in action, that by his living he may point out the way of life to those who are put under him . . . and that . . . [those under him] may learn how to walk rather through example than through words. . . .

The ruler ought also to understand how commonly vices pass themselves off as virtues. . . . It is necessary for the ruler of souls to distinguish . . . between virtues and vices . . . ; or, in overlooking what he ought to have smitten [criticized], he draw on those that are under him to eternal punishment; . . . or, by putting off the merit of a good action, change it to something worse. . . .

Let us now set forth after what manner [the priest] should teach. . . . For, . . . one and the same exhortation [instruction] does not suit all . . . [because] all are not bound together by similarity of character. For the things that profit some often hurt others. . . . Therefore, . . . the discourse [lecture] of teachers . . . [should] be fashioned . . . to suit all and each for their several needs, and yet never deviate the art of common edification [instruction]. . . .

We are brought back by the earnest desire . . . that every preacher should give forth a sound [he should provide a model] more by his deeds than by his words, and rather by good living imprint footsteps for men to follow than by speaking show them the way to walk."

Pope Gregory established rules of conduct for priests.

men and their visions, prophecies, and miracles; and the *Magna moralia,* a six-volume study of the book of Job. His work was filled with speculation about angels, demons, purgatory, penance, miracles, and holy relics—all subjects that would cram the pages of later medieval religious works.

Besides his concern with church reform, Gregory also had to worry about Rome's neighbors to the north and south. With the collapse of the Ostrogothic kingdom, a new set of Germans, the Lombards, had marched into northern Italy, and to the south were the Byzantine forces that had stayed in Italy after pushing the Ostrogoths out. Technically, these latter were Gregory's allies. In reality, he could not count on them "in view of the mutually exclusive claims to be the vicar of God

Pope Gregory was the first strong pope of the Middle Ages. He lived simply and in poverty, even after his papal election, and enthusiastically reformed many church policies.

on Earth made by the pope and the [Byzantine] emperor," according to author Norman F. Cantor.[25]

Indeed, Gregory had good reason to distrust the Byzantine Empire. In a 591 letter to the Byzantine emperor Maurice, and quoted by C. Warren Hollister, Gregory complains that he and others are being blamed for a Lombard attack on Rome, which resulted in many citizens' being captured and sold as slaves in the former imperial province of Gaul:

> The peace [with the Lombards] having been broken, the [imperial] soldiers were removed from the Roman city. . . . After this a still heavier blow was the arrival of Agilulph [the Lombard king and his army], so that I saw . . . Romans tied by the neck with ropes like dogs to be taken to Gaul for sale. And, because we in the city . . . escaped [Agilulph's] hand, a reason was then sought for making us look culpable [guilty]. . . . On my own account, I was in no way disturbed. . . . But for the glorious men, . . . the praefect [mayor of Rome] and . . . the military commander [of Rome], I have been distressed to a great degree, seeing that they did not neglect to do all that could be done. . . . As to them, I clearly understand that it is not their conduct but my person [their association with Gregory] that goes against them. For having along with me labored in trouble, they are alike troubled after labor.[26]

Thus, convinced that the soldiers of the Byzantine Empire would not protect Rome from the Lombards, Gregory used money generated by rent from church-owned buildings and from the sale of crops from church-owned farms to raise and pay for an army. By having his own army, Gregory made the papacy and Rome into one of the most powerful states in western Europe, and he made the position of pope not only head of the western church, but also the civil ruler of Rome.

In hopes of finding more reliable allies than the Byzantines, Gregory contacted the Franks, another group of Germans, who had carved a large kingdom out of the former Roman province of Gaul and who, unlike most German Christians, belonged to the church of Rome. Nothing came of Gregory's effort, but his attempt would lead to later contact and alliance between the western church and the Frankish kingdom. That alliance would eventually pull the church of Rome completely away from the Byzantine church and link its fortunes to the young western kingdoms of Europe.

The Monastic Movement

Pope Gregory I was the product of the most important movement in the Early Middle Ages church, monasticism. Monasticism was a reaction against what some Christians saw as the loss of spiritual values within the church, as author David Nicholas explains:

> As the church prospered . . . , many thoughtful Christians were disturbed by the changes that the church had undergone . . . , particularly its growing wealth. Far from attempting to escape the snares of the world, church leaders sought to strengthen their position . . . by accumulating wealth. . . . A growing number of persons . . . sought to escape the material world by living in isolation

as hermits. . . . Partly in reaction against the theatrical asceticism [self–denial] of some hermits, the . . . monastic form of the solitary life . . . developed. . . . In contrast to hermits . . . monks lived in communities with a common aim of avoiding materialism and temptation, but they avoided the dangers inherent in total isolation.[27]

The rules of monastic orders required that the monks follow strict rules and normally give up all possessions, including property, money, and personal clothing. They spent much of their time at religious worship and the rest working to make the monastery as self-sufficient as possible. In the east, those in monasteries had virtually nothing to do with the outside world. Officials in these eastern monasteries were often extremely active in church politics but never secular politics.

However, western monks, although always living separately from the rest of society, were never so isolated. First, charity was held to be such an important virtue that western monks had to deal with the outside world: "if we wish to dwell . . . in his [God's] kingdom, we will not reach it unless we approach by our good deeds," wrote the monk Saint Benedict.[28] Thus, monks took care of the sick and provided homes for orphans. Second, western monks proved to be among the most effective missionaries, converting many in northern Europe to Christianity. Finally, according to historian Crane Brinton, "as scholarship became one of the recognized forms of the monk's labor, the monasteries . . . [became] the guardians of the western intellectual heritage."[29] Such scholarly activity eventually led many monasteries to start schools.

Although monks were part of the clergy, they did not have a place in the church hierarchy. Bishops were technically in charge of supervising monasteries, but they and the monasteries' abbots were often at odds with one another. Part of the conflict arose because priests saw themselves as active Christians, soldiers of God—literally, at times—and believed that the monks were dodging their Christian duties by retreating from the world. The monks, on the other hand, believed that they were purer and closer to God than any priest or bishop because of that very isolation from the world. Most of these difficulties were eliminated by having the abbots sit on various church councils and by the election to pope of Gregory the Great, a former monk.

The Benedictines

Western monasticism was shaped by Benedict of Nursia who, in 529, established a monastery in southern Italy on Monte Cassino. Benedict created such a workable model for running a monastery that it was used by most of the western monastic orders of the Early Middle Ages. Besides the usual requirements for monastic life, the Rule of Saint Benedict, the document in which the monk explains his plan, insists on strict discipline and complete obedience to the monastery's regulations. The rule also says that the monastery should be run by an abbot, or chief monk, elected for life. According to the rule, as quoted by Will Durant, the abbot "shall make no distinction of persons in the monastery. . . . A freeborn man shall not be preferred to one coming from servi-

The Benedictine order of monks established the modern idea of a monastery.

tude. . . . God is no respecter of persons."[30]

The Benedictine monasteries that were later established provided many important services to the regions in which they were located. They managed the only hospitals and orphanages in much of Europe during this period. They were also a major civilizing force in the Early Middle

Saint Benedict Describes a Monk's Life

Saint Benedict laid out what he believed the monastic life should be and how monks should conduct themselves in his Rule, a document that became the blueprint for western medieval monastic orders. Here, he describes some of the requirements of the monk's life as quoted in A Source Book of Medieval History.

"33. *Whether the monks should have anything of their own.* More than anything else is this special vice to be cut off root and branch from the monastery, that one should presume to give or receive anything without the order of the abbot, or should have anything of his own. He should have absolutely not anything, neither a book, nor tablets [on which to write], nor a pen—nothing at all. For indeed it is not allowed to the monks to have their own bodies or wills in their own power. But all things necessary they must expect from the Father of the monastery. . . . All things shall be held in common. . . . If anyone shall have been discovered delighting in this most evil vice . . . let him be subjected to punishment. . . .

48. *Concerning the daily manual labor.* Idleness is the enemy of the soul. And therefore . . . the brothers [monks] ought to be occupied in manual labor; and . . . sacred reading. . . . If the . . . poverty of the place demands that they be occupied in picking fruits, they shall not be grieved; for they are truly monks if they live by the labors of their hands. . . .

53. *Concerning the reception of guests.* All guests . . . shall be received as though they were Christ . . . but most of all to servants of the faith and to pilgrims. . . .

54. *Whether a monk should be allowed to receive letters or anything.* By no means shall it be allowed a monk—either from his relatives, or from any man, or from one of his fellows—to receive or to give, without order of the abbot, letters, presents, or any gift, however small."

St. Benedict speaks with another monk and nuns.

St. Benedict in prayer. The monasteries founded by Benedict reached out into neighboring communities, managing orphanages, hospitals, and, eventually, setting up the first schools.

Ages, providing an example of order and discipline, preserving classical works, and teaching reading and writing. It was this last activity that may have been their most important contribution to Early Middle Ages culture because some 90 percent of those who could read and write in the five centuries following the fall of Rome were taught in Benedictine schools.

The Church and the Classical Heritage

Although the church did preserve Roman and Greek books and art, it never saw such preservation as part of its mission. Indeed, the attitude of the clergy to the west's classical past was mixed. While most found Roman books useful in teaching Latin, many were horrified at the constant references to Roman gods and goddesses in this material, as well as at the explicit sexual content of much Roman poetry and drama. Further, say historians Knowles and Obolensky:

It was perhaps natural to feel hostility towards a literature which was the principal attraction of a way of life that could still pose as a rival to Christianity and which was permeated [filled throughout] by the spirit of worldly splendor [richness].[31]

The result of this hostility was often the removal of offensive passages.

Gregory the Great went even further. He did not want anything to do with Roman and Greek writing, preferring instead original Latin works that had nothing but Christian thought in them. Gregory may or may not have destroyed classical texts, as some Christians certainly did, but as pope, he did forbid the teaching of most Roman and Greek works in church schools. Monastery-run schools also taught "exclusively [only] devotional material," and efforts "to graft classical studies onto monastic education [were] unsuccessful," notes historian David Nicholas.[32]

On the other hand, some clergy, like Isidore, who became the archbishop of Seville while Gregory was still pope, almost worshiped ancient Roman and Greek works. And even the strictest Christians admired the work of the Roman poet Virgil, author of the epic poem *Aeneid*. These Christians believed that a passage in his collection of poetry *Eclogues* referred to the birth of Christ. In the Early Middle Ages Virgil came to be seen by some as a prophet with magical powers, and out of this belief grew a group of legends portraying him as the great magician, Virgil Magus. Later, in the fourteenth century, this reverence toward Virgil would lead the Italian writer Dante to use the Roman poet as his fictional guide through hell in *The Divine Comedy*.

The church did have numbers of Roman and Greek books, as well as art-work, and if its clergy were unconcerned about, or even openly hostile to, much of this material, others were not. Although the number of people interested in this classical heritage, even among the nobility of the new German states, would remain small during the Early Middle Ages, some western Europeans would seek out these classical remains. And, in the growing kingdom of the Franks, such interest and such seeking would create, if only for a short time, a very real rebirth of learning and art.

While many Greek and Roman works were condemned by the clergy, the works of Virgil (pictured) were generally admired. Some clergy even thought that Virgil predicted the birth of Christ.

3 Kingdom and Empire in the West: The Franks

At the same time that Theodoric the Great and his Ostrogoths were setting up their Italian kingdom, other Germans were carving out kingdoms of their own. To the west the Visigoths were pushing into Spain, and to the north and west the Franks were conquering the Roman province of Gaul, while the Angles, Saxons, and Jutes were overrunning the island of Britain. The conquest of Gaul and Britain would be important to the development of the Late Middle Ages and the modern Western world. However, in the Early Middle Ages, the Franks would have the most impact on the rest of western Europe.

Under the leadership of their kings, such as Clovis, Pépin the Short, and Charlemagne, the Frankish state expanded. Eventually the Franks created a short-lived empire with a minor reawakening of art and learning. Out of the breakup of the Frankish empire would emerge France and Germany.

The First Merovingian King

The Franks began an expansion from their home around A.D. 431 along the Rhine, in what is now the Netherlands, Belgium, and the Rhineland portion of Germany. Divided into two groups, the Salian (those living near the sea) and the Ripuarian (those living near the Rhine and Meuse Rivers), they raided toward the south. Unlike a lot of German tribes, however, the Franks never moved out of their original homeland. They just added to it.

In 481 Clovis, the fifteen-year-old son of a Frankish chieftain, inherited the lead-

At the age of fifteen, Clovis became the leader of the Salian Franks. In twenty-five years, he defeated the last Roman army in Gaul, taking control of Gaul and much of western Europe.

ership of the Salian Franks. Although young, Clovis was both ambitious and able, and over the next twenty-five years he defeated the last Roman army in Gaul and beat off the attack of another German tribe, the Allemanni. His two victories left the Franks in control of Gaul and rulers of much of western Europe from the North Sea to the Pyrenees. In 509 Clovis declared himself king of all the Franks and their territory, thus becoming the first of the Merovingian line of kings.

Like many other German barbarians, Clovis converted to Christianity. However, unlike the Goths and the Lombards, Clovis joined the church of Rome. Because he practiced the same brand of Christianity as the priests and bishops in Gaul, he gained their support, as well as that of the people of the conquered Roman province.

Although Clovis ruled over a large kingdom, he did not leave the whole to a single heir. Instead, he followed the German custom of dividing his holdings among his four sons upon his death. This particular custom would remain popular with Frankish rulers throughout the Early Middle Ages.

The Mayors of the Palace

Almost upon Clovis's death, the Merovingians began a struggle to reunite the now divided Frankish kingdom. Such struggles would plague the descendants of Clovis and would lead them to plot and counterplot against one another. The Merovingians would stoop to every form of treachery, including assassination. Gregory of Tours, a sixth-century historian,

describes how Fredegund, wife of Clovis's grandson, used murder and torture in an attempt to make herself queen. After having her stepson assassinated, Fredegund turned on her own daughter, Rigunth, who was now a rival:

Sometimes [Fredegund and Rigunth] even came to blows. . . . One day her mother said to her: "Why dost thou set thyself against me, O my daughter? Here are possessions of thy father which I have under my control; take them and do with them as seemth good to thee." [Fredegund] then went into her treasure-room, and opened a chest full of necklets and precious ornaments, for a long time taking out one thing after another, and handing them to her daugher, who stood by. At last [Fredegund] said: "I am weary; put thou in thy hand, and take out what thou mayst find." Rigunth put her arm into the chest to take out more things, when her mother seized the lid and forced it down upon her neck. She bore upon it with all her strength, until the edge of the chest pressed beneath the girl's throat. . . . The attendants outside . . . broke into the small chamber, and brought out the girl, whom they thus delivered from . . . death.[33]

The last of the Merovingian kings were called the do-nothing kings because they spent their lives isolated in their castles while palace officials actually ran the kingdom. The most powerful of these officials came to be known as the mayor of the palace, a position roughly like that of prime minister in present-day Great Britain. In the early eighth century one of these mayors of the palace, Charles

Martel, became king in all but name. His descendants would found the Carolingian line of kings, a name that comes from *Carolus*, the Latin word for *Charles*.

Charles Martel turned the Franks into a highly effective cavalry force, and his military strategy of delivering hard blows to the enemy earned him his nickname, Charles the Hammer. It was this cavalry and these hard blows that, in 732, defeated a Muslim army at Tours. The Muslims, followers of Islam, had conquered Spain some twenty years earlier and were now beginning to probe farther north into Europe. However, after their defeat at Tours, the Muslims never again ventured north of the Pyrenees, the mountains that separate Spain from the rest of Europe.

While Charles Martel did not call himself king of the Franks, his son Pépin the Short did, becoming the first Carolingian king in 751. Twelve years later, Pope

Charles Martel (mounted) united the Franks into a highly effective cavalry force. Nicknamed Charles the Hammer because of his aggressive tactics, Charles defeated a Muslim army at Tours in 732.

*Pépin the Short became the
first Carolingian king in 751.*

Stephen II visited Pépin, now Pépin III, and asked for the king's help in controlling the Lombards, whose recent conquests were coming alarmingly close to Rome. The pope's request was the same as that made of the Franks by Pope Gregory I 150 years earlier. This time, however, the Franks and the church joined forces.

In exchange for the pope's approval of Pépin's having taken the crown from the Merovingians, the Frankish king agreed to fight the Lombards. The pope's support, as well as the ceremony at which Pépin was anointed with oil by the pope's representative, so impressed the Franks that any questions about the Carolingians' right to the throne were silenced forever.

After this ceremony Pépin defeated the Lombards in two campaigns and gave part of their kingdom to the papacy. This land gift, known as the Donation of Pépin, was combined with the territory surrounding Rome to form the Papal States, which lasted well into the nineteenth century.

The successful alliance of the papacy with the Frankish kingdom clinched the pope's long-sought goal of independence. Now, the Franks' powerful military saw to it that no one, Lombard king or Byzantine emperor, would conquer and impose his rule on the pope. Nor was it likely that the Franks themselves would take over Rome. They were too busy with their growing kingdom, by this time the largest governed region in the west since the fall of the Roman Empire. Additionally, in creating this kingdom, the Franks had made a lot of enemies and needed the goodwill of the popes in their dealings with these enemies.

The Emperor Charlemagne

The greatest of the Carolingians was Pépin's son Charlemagne, who ruled from 771 to 814. The name Charlemagne came from the Latin *Carolus Magnus*, that is,

An idealized painting of Charlemagne as a powerful warrior-king.

Charles the Great. Under Charlemagne the Frankish state reached its greatest extent, covering most of western Europe and becoming an empire. Charlemagne was also responsible for a reawakening of art and learning during his time as ruler of the Franks.

One of Charlemagne's first acts upon becoming king was to finish the conquest of the Lombards that his father had begun. Then he turned his attention east, and in 785, after almost a decade of truly bloody war, he defeated the Saxons and added what is now modern Germany to his kingdom. Charlemagne converted the Saxons to Christianity, although most of the converts accepted the church only after being threatened with death.

Between his western territory and eastern Europe, Charlemagne set up frontier provinces that he called marches to protect the eastern Frankish state. These marches also provided bases for the occasional Frankish military expedition into eastern Europe, for although the Franks did not have the resources to conquer this eastern land, they considered it to be under their protection. This belief on the Franks' part that eastern Europe was theirs led to centuries of German aggression in eastern Europe, which came to be called the *Drang nach Osten*, meaning *the drive toward the east*, and which was last seen as recently as World War II.

Charlemagne was not as successful in his campaign in Spain as he was against the Lombards and the Saxons. Although he set up a march on the southern side of the Pyrenees, he was unable to take and hold any land controlled by the Muslims, who occupied most of the Spanish peninsula.

Even without Spain Charlemagne's kingdom was immense for the time. It ran a thousand miles east from the western coast of Europe to the Elbe River and almost as far from the North Sea to the Mediterranean. It covered an area one-fifth the size of the continental United States and included all of modern-day France, Switzerland, the Low Countries, and much of today's Germany and Austria, as well as running deep into northern Italy.

On Christmas Day in 800, Pope Leo III crowned Charlemagne emperor of the western Roman Empire, even though the Frankish state did not cover quite the same lands as the old empire and even though the Byzantine emperors still claimed to be the only Roman emperors. It was a title that Charlemagne had not

A Portrait of the Emperor

What sort of man was Charlemagne, whose fifty years as king and emperor overshadow the accomplishments of every other historical figure in the Early Middle Ages? In his Life of Charles the Great, *Charlemagne's secretary Einhard provides a detailed and fairly honest picture of the man who generated so many legends and tales, as quoted in* A Source Book of Medieval History.

"Charles was large and strong . . . though not . . . tall . . . his eyes very large and animated . . . hair auburn. . . . His appearance was always . . . dignified . . . , although his . . . [stomach was] prominent. . . . He took frequent exercise on horseback . . . and often indulged in swimming. . . .

He sometimes carried a jeweled sword, but only on great feast-days . . . . He despised foreign costumes, however handsome. . . . On great feast-days he made use of embroidered clothes . . . ; but on other days his dress differed little from ordinary people. . . .

Charles had the gift of ready and fluent speech, and could express whatever he had to say with the utmost clearness. He . . . [gave] attention to the study of foreign languages, and . . . was such a master of Latin that he could speak it as well as his own native tongue. . . . He was so eloquent . . . that he might have been taken for a teacher of oratory [speech]. . . . He took lessons in grammar. . . . The king spent much time and labor . . . studying. . . . He learned to make calculations . . . . He also tried to write, and used to keep tablets [for writing] . . . in bed under his pillow. . . .

He cherished with the greatest fervor and devotion the principles of the Christian religion. . . . He was a constant worshipper . . . , going morning and evening. . . .

He was very active in aiding the poor. . . . He not only . . . [gave] in his own country and his kingdom, but . . . [also to] Christians living in poverty in Syria, Egypt, and Africa. . . . He sent great and countless gifts to the popes; and . . . the wish that he had nearest his heart was to reestablish the ancient authority of the city of Rome . . . and to defend and protect the Church."

wanted, for as his secretary and biographer Einhard wrote, "had he [Charlemagne] known the intention of the Pope, he would not have entered the Church on that day."[34] Apparently Charlemagne was surprised by the pope as the two were

On Christmas Day in 800, Pope Leo III unexpectedly crowned Charlemagne emperor of the western Roman Empire as the two were kneeling and praying side by side.

kneeling and praying side by side at the Christmas service. Leo suddenly stood up and unexpectedly placed a crown on Charlemagne's head. Once crowned in public, Charlemagne could not easily refuse the title without causing a major break between himself and the pope. Pope Leo III apparently wanted a western emperor because such a ruler was one more defense against the demands of the Byzantine emperor.

But the title certainly did Charlemagne little good. As emperor, the Frankish chief soon found himself at war with the Byzantines over a title that he had not wanted.

The Division of Empire

Charlemagne, like the Merovingian king Clovis, had intended to divide his empire among his three sons, but when he died in

814, only his son Louis of Aquitaine was still alive. When Louis, known as the Pious, died in 840, he left the empire to his oldest son, Lothair, who became emperor and who was to rule the entire Frankish empire with his two surviving brothers, Charles the Bald and Louis the German, assisting him as kings in the west and east. Louis the Pious had made these plans years before his death:

> It pleased us [Louis the Pious] . . . to crown [Lothair] . . . with the imperial diadem [crown], and to appoint him our . . . successor to the Empire. . . . It was . . . agreed to confer upon his brothers . . . the title of King, and to determine the places . . . in which . . . they shall wield power under their elder brother. . . .
>
> 3. We wish the two brothers who bear the title of King to have power of their own to distribute all honours within their dominion. . . .

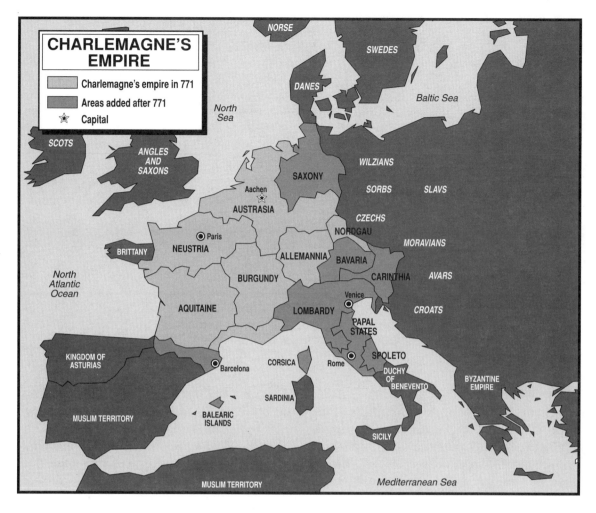

CHARLEMAGNE'S EMPIRE

	Charlemagne's empire in 771
	Areas added after 771
☆	Capital

NORSE

SWEDES

Baltic Sea

DANES

North Sea

SCOTS

ANGLES AND SAXONS

SAXONY

WILZIANS

SORBS

SLAVS

Aachen ☆

AUSTRASIA

CZECHS

NORDGAU

MORAVIANS

BRITTANY

Paris ◉

NEUSTRIA

ALLEMANNIA

BAVARIA

North Atlantic Ocean

BURGUNDY

CARINTHIA

AVARS

AQUITAINE

Venice ◉

LOMBARDY

CROATS

PAPAL STATES

KINGDOM OF ASTURIAS

Barcelona ◉

CORSICA

Rome ◉

SPOLETO

DUCHY OF BENEVENTO

BYZANTINE EMPIRE

SARDINIA

MUSLIM TERRITORY

BALEARIC ISLANDS

SICILY

MUSLIM TERRITORY

Mediterranean Sea

4. Again we wish them [the younger brothers], once a year . . . , to go to their elder brother with gifts . . . and in mutual brotherly love discuss vital matters and those connected with the common welfare and everlasting peace.[35]

However, the two younger brothers did not want to serve under Lothair. They, therefore, united and in front of their combined armies swore allegiance to each other. In order to be understood by all the soldiers present, they had to repeat their oaths first in the western Frankish lan-guage and then in the eastern. By the middle of the ninth century, western Frankish was already clearly changing into French and eastern Frankish into German.

In 843, after a year-long civil war, Charles and Louis forced Lothair to sign the Treaty of Verdun, which divided the Frankish empire into three parts. The treaty gave Charles the Bald a large region that would become France within a few centuries. Louis the German received a similarly sized territory that would one day become Germany. Lothair, the emperor, was left with a thin strip of territory that

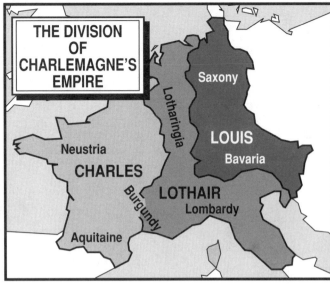

THE DIVISION OF CHARLEMAGNE'S EMPIRE

Saxony

Lotharingia

LOUIS

Neustria

Bavaria

CHARLES

LOTHAIR

Burgundy

Lombardy

Aquitaine

Charlemagne's son Louis meant for his son Lothair (left) to rule jointly with his brothers Charles and Louis. But the two did not want to serve with Lothair and forced him to sign the Treaty of Verdun, which divided the empire into three parts (right).

ran north and south between the much larger kingdoms of his two brothers. This imperial strip would be caught in a tug-of-war between the other two kingdoms, and even after the strip ceased to be a single state, it would remain a prize over which France and Germany would fight for centuries, even up into the twentieth century.

The result of the Treaty of Verdun was the loss of whatever unity the Frankish empire had gained during its short existence. The division of Charlemagne's empire was

The part of the empire that Charles the Bald (center) would rule would become France in a few centuries.

The three brothers announce the Treaty of Verdun, which would divide the Frankish empire forever after.

unavoidable because, observes author Crane Brinton, "nothing so large . . . could be maintained then [the Early Middle Ages]. The political, economic, and psychological bases for such . . . simply did not exist."[36] Further, as historian Norman F. Cantor points out, the Carolingian empire simply did not have enough talented and committed leaders to survive: "The death of only a few enlightened leaders, or even the sudden loss of one great personality, can cause the whole system to collapse and open the way for . . . [a rapid] reversion to chaos and barbarism."[37]

The Carolingian Renaissance

The sixth, seventh, and eighth centuries of the Early Middle Ages had seen a dramatic decrease in the production of art, music, and literature in western Europe. In part this decline was due to the economic collapse that followed the fall of the western Roman Empire. Fewer ways of making money, particularly through trade, meant fewer wealthy people, those whom artists, musicians, and writers had depended on in the ancient world to buy or pay for artistic work and whom creative people would continue to depend on even into modern times. In the opening centuries of the Early Middle Ages, those who passed for wealthy aristocrats in the German kingdoms had no time for art and learning. Their only object in life was to wage war.

Only the western church had the money to support art, but the church saw much of classical art and literature as sinful. Eventually religious art and writing would be important creative outlets, but not in the first centuries of the Early Middle Ages, when the church was more interested in the practical matters of survival and expansion.

Another reason for the decline in the various arts during the first half of the Early Middle Ages was that techniques and methods needed to paint, sculpt, compose music, and write poetry were often lost. Being able to do these things well, or even at all, generally requires training, and in the social chaos following the breakup of the Roman Empire, students found it impossible even to know who and where the teachers were. Thus, with the death of each generation, important skills were not passed along and were lost.

Charlemagne's Instructions on Education

The following letter, quoted in A Source Book of Medieval History, *was written by Charlemagne sometime before 800 and sent to Abbot Baugulf of the monastery at Fulda. Charlemagne reveals his belief that the clergy should have the necessary learning to make their religious teachings more trustworthy and effective and that education's major role should be to support religion. His views are very much in line with those of Pope Gregory I of two hundred years before.*

"Monasteries . . . , in addition to the order of monastic life and the relationships of holy religion, should be zealous also in the cherishing of letters [reading and writing] and in teaching those who . . . are able to learn, according as each has capacity. So that . . . those who wish to please God by living rightly should not fail to please Him also by speaking correctly. . . . For it is written, 'Either from thy words thou shall be justified or from thy words thou shalt be condemned.' . . . Although right conduct may be better than knowledge, nevertheless knowledge goes before conduct. . . . While errors should be shunned by all men, so much the more ought they to be avoided . . . by those [the clergy] who are chosen for this very purpose alone. They ought to be the specially devoted servants of truth. . . . In recent years when letters have been written to us from monasteries, . . . we have recognized . . . both correct thoughts and uncouth [incorrect] expressions. . . . We began to fear that . . . , as the skill of writing was less, so also the wisdom for understanding the Holy Scriptures [of the Bible] might be much less than it rightly ought to be. And we all know that, although errors of speech are dangerous, far more dangerous are errors of the understanding. . . .

Since . . . images [figures of speech] . . . and like figures are found in the sacred pages, nobody doubts that each one in reading these will understand the spiritual sense more quickly if previously he shall have been fully instructed in the mastery of letters. Such men truly are to be chosen for the work as have both the will and the ability to learn and a desire to instruct others."

However, it was not just artistic skills that were lost. More basic learning, such as reading, writing, and calculating, also disappeared among most people in western Europe. Again, it was a case of too few teachers with the necessary knowledge. Additionally, such education generally had little value among the younger German kingdoms, whose leaders could not see any use in being able to write or figure.

Charlemagne, however, realized that the survival of his kingdom depended on such basic skills as writing and calculating because someone had to keep the kingdom's records and accounts. Without such written records there was no way to know even the most basic things about the kingdom, such as how much money the state had. And so, with the aid of the English monk Alcuin, Charlemagne set up schools in order to educate the Franks, or at least the Frankish nobles. One of these schools was at the palace, and Charlemagne himself attended classes. This period of reawakened interest in learning is known as the Carolingian renaissance, or rebirth.

Alcuin had been the head of the most advanced school in western Europe—the cathedral school of York—a sort of early university. Recruited by Charlemagne in 781, he helped the Frankish ruler lure other teachers from Italy, England, and Spain. Next to Charlemagne, Alcuin was the most important person in the Carolingian renaissance, for as Norman F. Cantor says, "The educational work of Alcuin was decisive for the ninth and tenth centuries. Never again would Europe face the perils of . . . the possible extinction of the Latin culture that they had been in danger of in the seventh century."[38]

One of the English monk's greatest achievements was introducing a new system of handwriting. The handwriting of the period was difficult to read because letters were poorly formed and words were often run together. Alcuin's system used small, clearly made, uniform letters that were easy to read and inserted spaces between words. The letters of this handwriting were so well done that they became the model for today's printed letters.

Charlemagne's renaissance also extended beyond education into art and literature. However, Carolingian works of these kinds mostly copied and imitated Latin models, with little originality being shown.

During this period architects reintroduced Roman design in buildings, and the standard Roman public building, the basilica, which is shaped like a cross, became the model for Carolingian buildings. Some original designs were added to the western end of churches, where the architect might place a large decorated front or twin towers on either side of the entrance.

Artists departed from the abstract patterns that were common in the first few centuries of the Early Middle Ages and began using more human figures. These paintings, however, were not realistic, as the figures wore Roman clothes and were

Charlemagne (left), with the aid of the English monk Alcuin, set up schools to educate the Frankish nobles. Next to Charlemagne, Alcuin was perhaps the most important person in preserving the Latin culture.

shown in awkward, artificial positions. This trend in painting would continue through the remainder of the Middle Ages.

Also, as historian David Nicholas reports:

> Some good Latin poetry was . . . composed, . . . making up in freshness and originality of expression what most of it lacked in profundity [intellectual depth]. Theodulf of Orleans . . . composed elegant lyrics in a classical mode. Walafrid Strabo . . . wrote light verses and a poem, "On Gardening," which combines . . . the beauties of the garden . . . with . . . classics [Roman and Greek] and religious symbolism.[39]

Although greatly reduced because Charlemagne's successors spent much time and energy warring against each other, the Carolingian renaissance continued even after the Frankish emperor's death. Raban Maur, who studied under Alciun, was a classical scholar who made the monastery school at Fulda the best in western Europe. Charlemagne's son, Louis the Pious, like his father, had a palace school, and the court of Charles the Bald, grandson of Charlemagne, was famous for its religious discussions and debates.

However, the efforts to restart education and art by Charlemagne, Alcuin, and other Carolingians did not set off a general western European renaissance. That would have to wait for the relatively more stable times of the eleventh and twelfth centuries.

Visigothic Spain

The Carolingian renaissance was not the only flourishing of art and learning in western Europe, although it was the most far-reaching. In the Visigothic kingdom of Spain in the seventh century, a similar renaissance occurred.

The seventh-century Visigoths controlled all of the Spanish peninsula and would be the last group to do so. In the future, the peninsula would be shared by Muslim and Christian kingdoms and later by the nations of Spain and Portugal. During their century and a half of conquest, the Visigoths abandoned Arianism and converted to the church of Rome. Their particular brand of Christianity had been extreme, and unlike other Christian states of the time, the Visigothic kingdom had refused to accept any other Christian sect or any non-Christian religion. Indeed, European anti-Semitism got its start in this Spanish kingdom that exiled all its Jews in 672. Visigothic Spain was also the only German kingdom in which the clergy determined who would be king, as historian Will Durant points out: "The bishops . . . became . . . the chief power in the state; . . . they dominated the nobles . . . in the ruling councils . . . ; and though the king's authority was theoretically absolute [total] . . . these councils elected him."[40]

Despite this unbending and narrow faith, the Visigoths had their own cultural renaissance. Art flourished, although it closely followed ancient Roman and Greek styles that were modified by Christian subjects. The Visigoths also started schools that taught the classics. Poetry was revived, although like that of the later Carolingians, it imitated ancient Latin verse.

The high point of Visigothic writing was the work of Isidore, archbishop of Seville. Isidore's goal was to collect all the knowledge that he could and write it down. However, just as was true of the writings of other medieval authors, much of Isidore's information was second- and thirdhand, and the Spanish bishop made no attempt to distinguish what was true and what was false. Thus, his work was spoiled by many errors. However, his writing was popular with the Visigoths, as well as with the rest of western Europe at the time, and remained popular throughout the entire Middle Ages.

The Legends of Charlemagne

Charlemagne became such a giant figure in western Europe during the fifty years of his rule that, even after his death, no one could forget him. Over the next few centuries, stories and legends grew up around the medieval monarch that heralded him as an almost superhuman leader. These legends mixed a little truth with a lot of imagination and created a never-never land filled with heroic knights, beautiful princesses, ogres, dragons, and villains. Like the more familiar King Arthur, the legendary Charlemagne was surrounded by a band of skilled and brave knights. The Charlemagne knights were called paladins and numbered twelve.

Even when the legends revolve around real happenings, they take great liberties with the truth. In 778, when Charlemagne left Spain, part of his army was attacked at Roncesvalles by Pyrenees Basques, who wiped out the entire rear guard. Among those killed was Roland, the governor of the march of Brittany. Roland was, at best, a minor figure in the history of the period. However, in the Charlemagne legends, he became the most famous of the

paladins, although his name was often changed to Orlando.

Roland's death and the battle of Roncesvalles are the subjects of one of the most famous medieval epics, *The Song of Roland*. However, this epic is in no way a history of the battle, because it departs from history quite dramatically. First, in *The Song of Roland*, Charlemagne is returning from having conquered all of Muslim Spain, whereas the real Frankish king never gained any land in Spain except for a small strip in the north. Second, in the poem, the attack at Roncesvalles is a conspiracy

Although Roland was only a minor figure in history, in the legends that followed Charlemagne's death he became a prominent hero in many medieval epics.

In legend only, Charlemagne conquers Jerusalem. These legends that followed Charlemagne's death heralded him as almost superhuman, as he and his heroic knights saved beautiful princesses from ogres and dragons.

between a villainous Frankish knight and the Muslims, whereas in reality, there was no conspiracy and the attackers were Basques, who were Christians like the Franks.

The Legacy of Charlemagne

Charlemagne's empire failed to replace the lost centralized government of Rome. Yet, the Frankish emperor was especially important to the Early Middle Ages because of his concern with law. One of Charlemagne's goals after becoming emperor was to reform the legal system in the Frankish state. As the emperor's biographer Einhard notes:

> When he had taken the imperial title he noticed many defects in the legal

systems of his people; for the Franks have two legal systems, differing in many points . . . from one another, and he, therefore, determined to add what was lacking, to reconcile the differences, and to amend anything that was wrong or wrongly expressed. . . . He gave orders that the laws and rules of all nations . . . within his domains which were not already written out should be collected and committed to writing.[41]

Although Charlemagne did not live to complete this plan, he did set legal reform in motion. As historian David Nicholas notes, "Although the unification of Europe . . . was a personal achievement that survived only a generation after his death, Charlemagne's transformation of local institutions [customs] was to survive . . . throughout the Middle Ages."[42] Among

Emperor Against Emperor

Although the eastern empire had recognized Charlemagne as emperor of the western empire, the Byzantines did not accept that this title could be inherited. In 871 Charlemagne's great-grandson, Emperor Louis II, defended his inherited right to the title in a letter to Basil I, the Byzantine emperor. This excerpt is quoted from Brian Pullan's Sources for the History of Medieval Europe, from the Mid-Eighth to the Mid-Thirteenth Century.

"It is ridiculous of you [Basil I] to say that the [western] imperial title is . . . [not] hereditary. . . . In what way is it not hereditary—for [my] grandfather was already inheriting it from his father. . . .

You profess to be astonished that we call ourselves Emperors, not of the Franks, but of the Romans: but . . . we could not be Emperors of the Franks without being Emperors of the Romans. We took over this title . . . from the Romans . . . ; and we received from heaven this people and this city [Rome] to guide and the mother of all churches of God to defend. . . . From her [the western church] the founder of our line received the authority, first to be King, and then to be Emperor. . . . And Charles the Great [Charlemagne] . . . was the first of our race and line . . . to be called Emperor. . . . Men have frequently risen to be Emperor . . . not by any divine operation carried out by the pontiff [pope], but only from the Senate and the people. . . . Some have not even risen by this means, for they have been . . . set upon the imperial throne by the soldiers, and some of them have even been promoted by . . . other dubious means. . . .

The Frankish race has borne the Lord much very fertile fruit, not only by being quick to believe, but also by converting others. . . . The Lord rightly warned you: 'The Kingdom of God shall be taken from you and given to a nation which bears him fruit.' . . . We have received the government of the Roman Empire for our right thinking. . . . The Greeks [Byzantines] for their . . . wrong thinking . . . have ceased to be Emperors of the Romans. . . . They have migrated to another capital city and taken up a completely different nationality and language."

the most important accomplishments of Charlemagne's reforms was the strengthening and refining of the feudal system, the political and economic system that was still in its infancy during the Frankish emperor's life and that would come to bind western European society together for the rest of the Middle Ages.

Chapter

4 The New Social Order: The Growth of Feudalism

Feudalism, or the feudal system, was the economic and political system under which western Europe operated through

An illustration from an illuminated manuscript depicts feudalism in action. Serfs tend the fields of a manor lord, who lives in the castle in the background.

much of the Middle Ages. It began to take shape toward the beginning of the Early Middle Ages, particularly under the first Frankish kings. By the time of Charlemagne the system existed in broad outline, with one noble promising to serve another, particularly in war, in exchange for certain rights, such as the use of land. As historian Crane Brinton says, its growth was in response to "the breakdown of . . . [people's] ability to hold together large groups of human beings for political or economic purposes. The One World of Roman law, administration, and business was shattered into hundreds, indeed thousands, of small local units."[43]

The Origins of Feudalism

The feudal system was not planned but, rather, grew and developed in response to the social chaos that followed the fall of the western Roman Empire. It provided order where there no longer was any, and it created new chains of command to replace those that were now gone. Under Rome the imperial bureaucracy had provided order for imperial society, and the central government in Rome had maintained that order through supervision and control. However, with the fall of the western empire, the means of preserving the imperial chains of command, which led from emperor and senate to province, city, and town, disappeared, and new ways of first forging and then maintaining new chains of command needed to be found during the Early Middle Ages. Feudalism did both.

Feudalism was of mixed heritage, some of it Roman, and some German. For example, the titles of count and duke came from Rome. Both ranks had originally been offices of imperial agents who oversaw the affairs of a local region. A count was in charge of a single county, while a duke supervised several counties. At the beginning of the Early Middle Ages, these titles were grabbed up by local landowners and became hereditary.

The organization of local feudal lords who ruled over country estates, which came to be called manors and which formed the core of Early Middle Ages society, were also adopted from Roman custom. Even before the final collapse of Rome, local landowners had been taking more care of those living on their properties.

German social customs also contributed to the growth of feudalism. As German immigrants and former Roman citizens mixed together in postimperial western Europe, so did their customs. Thus, in the first centuries of the Early Middle Ages, the former Roman country estates began taking on features of German villages.

Additionally, the German *comitatus* (retinue, or followers) became an important part of feudalism. The members of each comitatus swore allegiance to the leader of the band, according to historian George B. Adams:

The *comitatus* . . . was a . . . personal relationship of mutual protection, service, and support, between a chief and certain men, . . . voluntarily entered into on both sides. . . . It was not regarded by the Germans as a mere business transaction of give and take, but was looked upon as conferring especial [special] honor on lord and man alike.[44]

The comitatus would change and develop into the central relationship of lord and vassal that bound the feudal system together.

Oaths of Fealty and Fiefs

Under feudalism, two nobles entered into an agreement. One, known as the vassal (from Celtic, meaning "servant"), pledged to carry out a number of duties, of which the most important was military service. In exchange for these services, the other noble, called the lord, or suzerain from the Latin *sursum*, meaning "upward", or "the one above," then provided the vassal with protection, as well as a way of taking care of such basic needs as food and clothing.

The pledge that the vassal gave was an oath of fealty, or fidelity. Among the seventh-century Franks, these oaths were fairly straightforward arrangements. As C. Warren Hollister reports, for food and clothing, the Frankish vassal promised loyalty to his lord:

To that magnificent lord. . . . Since it is known . . . to all how little I have whence [with which] to feed and clothe myself, I have therefore petitioned your piety [goodness], and your good will has decreed to me that

A king receives a knight who is one of his vassals. Knights swore allegiance to nobles, who in turn swore allegiance to a king.

I should hand myself over . . . to your guardianship, which I have therefore done; that is to say . . . , that you should aid me . . . as well as with food as with clothing, according as I shall be able to serve you and deserve it.

And so long as I shall live I ought to provide service and honor to you, [acceptable] to my free condition, and I shall not during the time of my life have the ability to withdraw from your power or guardianship. . . . It is proper that if either of us shall wish to withdraw himself from these agreements, he shall pay . . . the other party, and this agreement shall remain unbroken.[45]

It was not long before Frankish lords were giving their vassals more than just the essentials. In exchange for fealty, the vassal received a benefice (from the Latin for "benefit"). The first benefices were given by the church to local nobles, but under the Carolingians, Frankish kings and nobles began handing them out as well. Eventually the word *benefice* was replaced by *fief* (meaning "fee"), from which the term *feudal* comes.

A benefice, or fief, was a grant that gave a vassal certain privileges. A vassal might be granted the use of a specific property of the lord, which could be anything from a single castle to an entire province. However, fiefs did not necessarily have anything to do with property, and a vassal's benefice might allow him to gather taxes, mint coins, or assign and collect fines. Some vassals, such as those knights who lived with a lord, received no fiefs at all.

A benefice was valuable, and its possession drew many nobles into vassalage. As the French historian F.L. Ganshof points out, the Carolingian kings were able to make vassals out of even the highest ranking Frankish nobles, dukes, and counts:

The Giving of a Benefice

As the feudal system developed, a vassal who owned land was required to give that land to his lord. The lord then returned the land to the vassal to hold as a benefice, or fief. In the first of two general documents below, a vassal gives up his land to his lord, in this case the abbot of a monastery, and then requests it back as a benefice. In the second document, the abbot grants the vassal the benefice. The documents are quoted in A Source Book of Medieval History.

"I . . . have settled in my mind that I ought . . . to make a gift from my possessions. . . . And this is what I hand over . . . , all those possessions of mine which . . . my father left me at his death, . . . or those which I was able afterward to add to them . . . , that is to say, the courtyard with its buildings, with slaves, houses, lands (cultivated and uncultivated), meadows, woods, waters, mills, etc. These . . . , with all things adjacent or belonging to them, I hand over to . . . the abbot. . . . On these conditions: that so long as life remains in my body, I shall receive from you as a benefice . . . the possessions above described. . . . And my son shall have the same possessions for the days of his life."

"Since it is not unknown how you [the vassal] . . . did grant to . . . [the abbot] . . . all your possessions which you seemed to have . . . , which your father on his death bequeathed [left] to you there, or which by your own labor you were able to gain there, . . . with courtyard and buildings, gardens and orchards, with various slaves, . . . houses, lands, meadows, woods (cultivated and uncultivated), or with all . . . belonging to it, which it would be extremely long to enumerate [list], in all their completeness; but afterwards, at your request, it seemed proper to us [the abbot] to cede to you the same possessions. . . . And if God should give you a son . . . , he shall have the same possessions for the days of his life."

The . . . Carolingians, by distributing as benefices to their vassals the wealth of . . . great estates . . . , attracted members of higher social levels into the ranks of their vassals. A steadily growing proportion of members of the aristocracy, including . . . the counts, were now prepared to become vassals of the king.[46]

Along with a fief, a lord often gave a vassal immunity, which let the vassal make his own laws and run his own courts. A fief and immunity were normally given in exchange for a vassal's

A tenant pays rent to his lord. Under feudalism, serfs were allowed to live on the land of a lord in exchange for work and a portion of the serf's crops.

contributing a certain number of soldiers to his lord's army.

The benefices or fiefs of early feudalism were not inherited, but by the end of the Early Middle Ages, they had become so. The vassal heir had to pay a form of inheritance tax, called relief, to his lord. This relief could be as much money as the fief produced in a year. For vassals who died without heirs, the fief was the lord's to dispose of as he saw fit.

Lords and Vassals

To be a vassal was an honor, and not one lightly given. Indeed, only members of the upper class were allowed to become vassals. Thus, nobles, such as dukes and knights, took the oath of fealty, but common soldiers did not. High-ranking church officials could also be vassals, according to Will Durant: "Archbishops, bishops, and abbots . . . pledged their fealty . . . , carried such titles as duke and count, minted coin, . . . and took on the feudal tasks of military service and agricultural management."[47] No one else, including the lower clergy, could be a vassal. Even among the upper class not everyone was a vassal, although most were.

Under feudalism both the lord and the vassal had duties and rights. A lord promised to protect his vassal and the vassal's fief, by going to war if necessary, and to see that a vassal accused of breaking his oath, or of any other crime, would have the chance to plead his case before his social equals, or peers.

In return, the vassal pledged to give advice, both to the lord and to other vassals of the lord. The vassal also promised to provide his lord with aid, particularly military. Thus, if his lord commanded, the vassal, fully equipped with armor and weapons, had to go to war. However, to keep warfare from being too time consuming and costly to the vassal, this military service was normally limited to forty days a year.

The vassal's aid might further require him to house and feed his lord, as well as the lord's entire household. Because roads were poor, it was often easier and more reliable for lords to go to the food rather than to have the food brought to them. Again, to keep this form of aid from becoming too heavy a burden, the lord's stay was limited.

The final form of aid that a vassal might have to provide was money when the lord needed it. Emergencies, long wars, or important events, such as the marriage of the lord's oldest daughter or the knighting of his oldest son, called for such financial aid.

The Duties of Both Lords and Vassals

In the following letter, written in 1020 and quoted in A Source Book of Medieval History, *Bishop Fulbert of Chartres spells out the duties of lord and vassal in the feudal system. The bishop makes it clear that the feudal relationship was not a one-way street and that a lord who failed to meet his responsibilities was every bit as bad as a vassal who failed in his.*

"He who takes the oath of fealty to his lord ought always to keep in mind these six things: what is harmless, safe, honorable, useful, easy, and practicable. *Harmless,* which means that [the vassal] ought not to injure his lord in his body; *safe,* that [the vassal] should not injure [the lord] by betraying his confidence [trust] or the defenses upon which he depends for security; *honorable,* that [the vassal] should not injure [the lord] . . . in matters that relate to [the lord's] honor; *useful,* that [the vassal] should not injure [the lord's] . . . property; *easy,* that [the vassal] should not make difficult that which his lord can do easily; and *practicable,* that [the vassal] should not make impossible for the lord that which is possible.

However, while it is proper that the faithful vassal avoid these injuries, it is not for doing this alone that he deserves his holding; for it is not enough to refrain from wrongdoing, unless that which is good is done also. . . . Therefore, . . . in the same six things referred to above he should faithfully advise and aid his lord, if he wishes to . . . be safe concerning his fealty which he has sworn.

The lord also ought to act toward his faithful vassal in the same manner in all these things. And if he fails to do this, he will be rightfully regarded as guilty of bad faith, just as the former [would be], if he should be found shirking . . . his obligations."

A king distributes royal charters to his vassals. Under feudalism, both lords and vassals had certain rights and responsibilities.

Both lords and vassals, as well as members of their households, came to believe that nothing was more important than being a good vassal to a lord. In the following letter, written in 843, a mother instructs her son on his behavior as vassal to the Carolingian king Charles the Bald:

> Since God . . . and your father have chosen you . . . to serve Charles as your lord, I urge you ever to remember the record of your family . . . and not to serve your master simply to satisfy him outwardly, but to maintain towards him and his service in all things a devoted and certain fealty both of body and soul. . . . I exhort [strongly urge] you to maintain faithfully all that is in your charge, with all your strength of body and soul, as long as your life shall last. . . . May the madness of infidelity be ever far from you; may evil never find such a place in your heart as to render you unfaithful to your lord in any matter whatsoever. . . . Therefore, my son . . . show yourself towards your lord . . . [as] true, vigilant, useful, and prompt to his service. In every matter which concerns the power and welfare of [your lord] . . . show that wisdom that God has plentifully endowed you.[48]

The bond between suzerain and vassal could be broken by a lord who found a vassal guilty of not meeting his duties. The lord then stripped the vassal of his fief, declaring that the vassal must "hand over and restore to us . . . all that land which you hold from us in fee [fief]."[49]

It was harder for a vassal to break the feudal contract. The early Frankish custom of letting a vassal buy his way out of service disappeared in the eighth century. By the ninth, it was illegal for a vassal to leave his lord except for such major violations of fealty as the lord's trying to kill his vassal.

It was also easier for a lord to find a new vassal than for a vassal to find a new lord. The lord had a fief with which to lure a new vassal, whereas a vassal who had left his suzerain generally had nothing to offer beyond what any number of other candidates possessed. Further, the former vassal was viewed with suspicion and distrust by possible lords.

The Feudal Hierarchy

The oath of fealty and the relationship of vassal to suzerain owed much of their existence to the German comitatus and the oaths sworn between German warriors and chiefs. In fact, the first vassals were no more than fighting men taken on by their lord to increase the strength of his private army. However, the relationship between lords and vassals, and consequently the feudal hierarchy, grew more complex as vassals became more than just soldiers in an army.

Nothing in the feudal system kept lords from being vassals to other nobles as well, nor kept vassals from being lords. In fact, most nobles were both, according to Ganshof:

> It is . . . very important to realize that vassals . . . with . . . estates of some magnitude would normally acquire other vassals for their own service. This would often . . . be done at their [own] lord's . . . desire, since in this way, they could raise a large number of fighting men for his service.[50]

In theory, the feudal hierarchy was shaped like a pyramid, with the king at the top. Below the king were his personal vassals, who were themselves lords to others below them. The pyramid continued on down until reaching vassals who had no vassals of their own.

In practice, however, feudalism was never so neat. First, the pyramid arrangement suggests that the higher a noble was in the feudal hierarchy, the more powerful he was. The reality was that vassals were often more powerful than their lords. In fact, it was not unusual for a king's vassals to be more powerful in land and in number of peasants loyal to them than he was.

Second, as feudalism evolved, some vassals gave oaths of fealty to more than one lord because they wanted the income from more than one fief. The result was that these nobles occupied different levels in the feudal hierarchy at the same time. These multiple oaths led to much confusion, particularly as to which lord should be served first. Often one lord was made the vassal's chief lord, who was called the liege lord—the one to whom he owed his first allegiance. Other reforms were also tried in attempts to straighten out feudal allegiances, but none worked very well.

In the end many nobles found that if they had enough soldiers, they did not have to concern themselves with oaths of fealty. Instead, they could simply go to war against other aristocrats, or nobles, and seize the properties desired. No amount of traditions, laws, court cases, or legal thinking put much of a stop to these private wars, which consumed much energy, time, and resources in both the Early and Late Middle Ages.

Carolingian Kings and Feudalism

A feudal king waged a constant battle to keep his vassals under his control. When a king lost that control, he became weaker than his vassals, who were then free to act as independently as they pleased. Charlemagne was aware of this danger. In an attempt to keep his authority over his vassals, he ordered that their first oath of fealty should be to him and not to their local lord. The Frankish king also tried to restrain vassals by sending around inspectors, known as *missi dominici* (Latin for "those sent out by the lord"). These missi dominici looked for nobles who were breaking the law and reported them to Charlemagne.

Charlemagne was not completely successful in controlling his fief holders. First, reports from his inspectors took a long time to reach him, particularly from the frontiers of his empire. Second, the Frankish ruler simply did not have the authority or power to make his vassals obey him if they chose not to. Charlemagne's ability to enforce orders to his vassals depended upon his military might, and Charlemagne's army was made up of his vassals and their soldiers. These Frankish vassals could not be fully trusted to back the emperor against one of their own.

The later Carolingian rulers fared even worse. The breakup of the Frankish empire led to increased warfare between various factions of the old state, as well as fighting with surrounding kingdoms. All of this took money and soldiers. The only way that the Frankish kings and emperors could get that money and those men was to make concessions to their various landholders.

Charlemagne receives the Oath of Fidelity and Homage from one of his High Barons (left). Charlemagne kept control of his vassals by making them pledge loyalty to him, rather than a local lord. (Below) The layout of a typical manor.

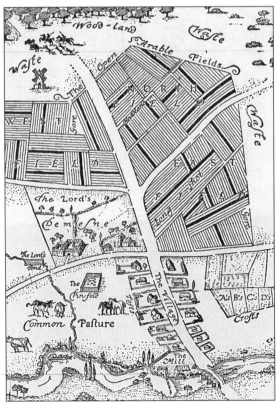

These concessions made fiefs hereditary and allowed the fief holders to become full feudal lords with the right to have their own vassals. By the end of the Early Middle Ages, what had been the Frankish empire was a collection of varying-sized feudal domains, which for all practical purposes operated as independent states.

The Manor

During the Early Middle Ages most Europeans lived and worked on farms. The majority of these farms in the west were part of a manor, or estate, many of which were originally Roman country estates. Manor size, population, and type of crops and animals raised differed, but in general each manor spread out from a large house or castle. Workers' cottages, as well as an occasional village within the estate, were surrounded by meadows, pastures, fields for growing crops, and woodlands.

Many medieval manors used what was called the three-field system for raising crops. Each year one field was used for spring planting, one for fall, and one was left unused. Use of the fields would rotate from year to year so that each field had time to rest and recover from being worked. The fields were divided into long strips, each separated from its neighbors by unplowed land. Fences were never used. The lord of the manor had a number of strips that provided food for his household.

Each manor supplied most of the needs of the people living on it, although not everything. As with any farming community, a manor sometimes had too much of some foods and not enough of others. Also, as the manor system grew, estates, just as farms do today, began specializing. Thus, some grew grain crops; others raised sheep, pigs, and cattle; and still others planted grapes for wine. From the excesses and shortages, as well as from specialization, trade between manors arose. As historian David Nicholas observes:

This manor would have been considered luxurious by medieval standards. Manors were virtually self-sufficient and provided for most of the needs of their occupants.

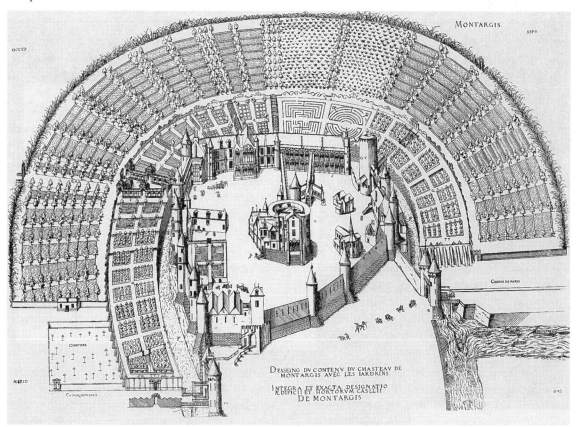

Trade was . . . necessary at all times. The fact that so many tenant farmers . . . were carrying products between estates suggests that villas [manors] were developing their own specialties and that the surplus of one would find a market on another [manor].[51]

The Lord of the Manor

The lord of the manor, or the landlord, was normally a vassal who was generally not the owner of the estate. The actual owner of the manor was probably not even the landlord's suzerain unless that lord were the king. A king supposedly owned all the land in his kingdom, and every landlord had use of that land either through direct or indirect vassalage to the king. In reality some land was always outside the feudal system and was privately owned by those living on it.

The landlord lived in the large house or castle on the grounds, if he stayed at his manor at all. His household included his family and other nobles, known as retainers. How much income the manor produced determined the size of the lord's household, which, in turn, set the number of soldiers that the landlord had to provide his suzerain.

Caring for the household were such servants as cooks, waiters, grooms, and huntsmen. Also, each manor had a priest, with rich manors having several, one of whom was assigned solely to the landlord's household.

The lord of the manor made money from his estate in a variety of ways, according to a quotation in Jonathan F. Scott's book, *Readings in Medieval History:*

Besides the produce [production] of livestock and crops . . . , the lord . . . had other sources of revenue. There were . . . the rents paid by . . . tenants . . . and the money . . . sometimes accepted in lieu [instead] of labour services. Sales of timber . . . , of turf . . . , licenses to fold [keep sheep] on the tenant's land, or . . . turn pigs into the lord's woods . . . , brought in varying sums of money. The mill at which the tenants ground their corn was [the landlord's] property. . . . A considerable portion of the tolls [fees for grinding corn] went into the landlord's purse. . . . On some manors the oven in which the bread was baked was also the property of the lord of the manor. The fees and fines levied [charged] by the manorial courts in the course of a year [were] surprisingly large. . . . Here were paid the fees . . . to reside outside the manor, to send children to school, . . . to apprentice a son to a trade, or to marry a daughter. Here, too, were imposed the fines for slovenly [sloppy] work . . . , for selling cattle without the lord's leave [permission], . . . for neglecting to repair a cottage. . . . Here the miller would be fined for mixing rubbish with his flour.[52]

Serfs and Other Peasants

Most of the inhabitants of the manor were peasants, known as tenants, the majority of whom were serfs (from the Latin *servus*, meaning "slave"). Serfs were mostly farmhands, although some did other jobs, such as blacksmithing. A serf depended on the lord of the manor for protection, and in partial payment for that protection he had to spend as much as half of every week working his landlord's fields. For this work, he was not paid. A serf often had to give part of his own crops to the lord of the manor and, upon inheriting his land, had to pay the lord a fee, known as heriot.

A serf had little freedom. Without his landlord's permission a serf could not leave the manor, could not change his job, and could not marry someone from another manor. For a serf's daughter to marry outside the manor, the serf not only had to get his landlord's consent but also had to pay a fine, called *merchet*. During the Middle Ages anyone who had to pay heriot and merchet was by definition a serf.

However, despite the serf's lack of freedom, a serf was not actually a slave. There were major differences between serfdom and slavery. First, a serf could not be bought and sold as could a slave. Second, by the end of the Early Middle Ages, a serf's position was as hereditary as was that of any noble, and his children and their children were also serfs, remaining on the same manor and farming the same land as had their father and grandfather. Third—and unlike any slave—a serf had certain rights. For example, he could not be stripped of his land as long as "he paid the rent [by supplying labor and food] and did the required services," according to Nicholas.[53]

The social contract between landlord and serf was not a feudal contract, and serfs were not vassals. Lord and vassal were always members of the upper class because feudal oaths could only be given and received by social equals, members of the nobility, and as Crane Brinton writes,

"the medieval aristocracy drew a sharp contrast between the honorable military aid of the vassal and the mere manual labor of the serf."[54]

In addition to the serfs, some of the manor's tenants were freemen, who enjoyed the full rights of citizenship and "who owned their land with little or no obligation to any feudal lord, or leased it from a lord for a money rent. . . . They probably constituted a quarter of the total peasant population in Western Europe."[55] There were also some landless workers among the manor's peasants.

An overseer watches over a serf who is building a road. Although serfs were tied to the manor on which they worked, they were not slaves.

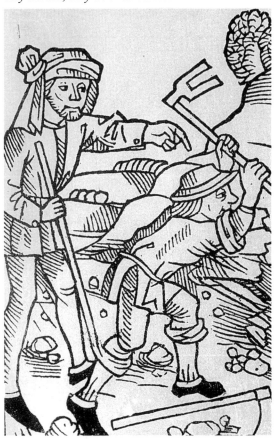

The Role of Women

The feudal system was concerned mostly with the rights of men. However, in some ways, western European women were better off in the Early Middle Ages than they had been under the Roman Empire. According to Nicholas, German custom allowed them to "inherit on the same basis as men. . . . The open society of early Frankish Gaul permitted some women to rise to positions of influence."[56] Still, a woman's rights in western Europe during the Early Middle Ages were generally tied to her being a wife or daughter, and although a woman could inherit her father's fief, she could do so only if she were married.

On the Early Death of a Vassal

The following instructions, quoted in A Source Book of Medieval History, *explain what to do with the children of a dead vassal if those children are too young to inherit. It also details what duties the vassal's lord must perform until the children are able to take over their father's fief.*

"Heirs should be placed in guardianship until they reach the age of twenty years; and those that hold them as wards should give over to them all the fiefs which came under their control by reason of wardship. . . .

When a female ward reaches the proper age to marry, she should be married by the advice and consent of her lord, and by the advice and consent of her relatives and friends, according as the nobility of her ancestry and the value of her fief may require; and upon her marriage the fief which has been held in guardianship should be given over to her. A woman cannot be freed from wardship except by marriage; and let it not be said that she is of age until she is twenty years old. But if she be married at the age at which it is allowable for a woman to marry, the fact of her marriage makes her of age and delivers her fief from wardship.

The fiefs of those who are under wardship should be cared for attentively by their lords, who are entitled to receive the produce and profits. And in this connection let it be known that the lord ought to preserve in their former condition the buildings, the manor-houses, the forests, and meadows, the gardens, the ponds, the mills, the fisheries, and the other things of which he has the profits. And he should not sell, destroy, or remove the woods, houses, or the trees."

Although a noble Frankish woman gained power mostly through marriage, she was guaranteed certain rights. She could inherit her father's fief and even run a manor while her husband was at war.

The only place where women were really in charge and could direct their own affairs was in a nunnery, the female counterpart to a monastery, although even here they were technically under the direction of a male bishop. Education was almost never available to women in medieval society, except to those who entered nunneries. The practices and education of women in nunneries was accepted because of the religious nature of these organizations and because of their isolation from the rest of society. Thus, the nunnery, as Norman F. Cantor writes, was a place of "moderate learning . . . and. . . . was the most continuing, least controversial, and universally admired" exception to the accepted role of women in medieval society.[57]

Even outside nunneries, some women achieved power during the Early Middle Ages. A few were wives who ran their husbands' estates while these men were at war, sometimes continuing that supervision even after the husbands' return. Some were women who married well, gaining power because of who their husbands were. Such a one was Theodora, wife of the Byzantine emperor Justinian I. Theodora, whose father had been a bear trainer, gained real political power when Justinian made her coruler of the Byzantine Empire.

5 Empire in the East: The Byzantines

While the Franks and other Germans were creating kingdoms out of the old western Roman Empire, the eastern Roman Empire, renamed the Byzantine Empire by modern historians, continued to exist. The east had survived when the west had not because, according to historian David Nicholas:

> Population density and . . . wealth were much higher in the east than in the west, making it less difficult to support the gigantic army and bureaucracy . . . [and] the eastern empire was more easily governable, centered on Asia Minor with a centrally located capital.[58]

Constantinople was the capital of the Byzantine Empire. Named for Emperor Constantine I who made it the capital of the eastern Roman Empire in the fourth century A.D., the city was also known as Byzantium, from the name of its legendary founder, Byzas. Throughout the Early and Late Middle Ages, Constantinople was called just the City. Its modern name, Istanbul, is nothing but a distortion of the Greek phrase meaning "to the city."

Constantinople sat on the European side of the Bosporus Straits—the middle section of the straits, which also includes the Sea of Marmara and the Dardanelles.

The straits link the Black Sea to the Mediterranean and divide Europe from Asia. The Byzantine capital was perfectly positioned for control of trade moving north and south through the straits and east and west across the Bosporus.

The Byzantines called themselves Romans because they always thought of themselves as the Roman Empire, and the Byzantine emperors believed themselves the direct heirs of the emperors of Rome. Yet to the kingdoms of western Europe, the empire was Greek, and indeed, by the end of the Early Middle Ages, the official language of the Byzantines was Greek, not Latin.

The Byzantine Emperor

The emperor was the absolute ruler of the Byzantine state, his power supposedly coming directly from God. In theory he was elected by the people, the senate, and the army, but this election quickly became a mere formality. No matter how powerful an emperor was, he could be dethroned and replaced, and over the centuries of the Early Middle Ages, various plots killed, imprisoned, and exiled emperors. Revolts were not unusual either.

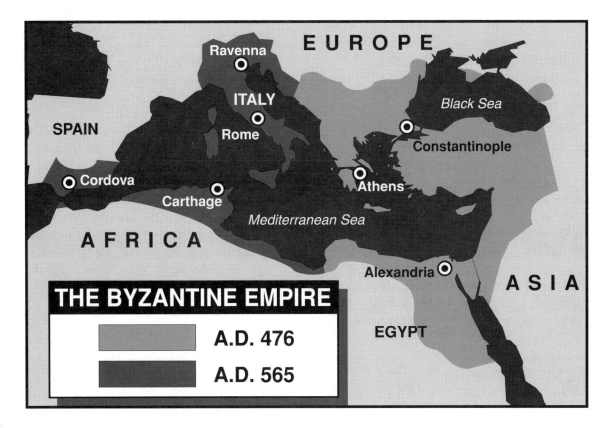

THE BYZANTINE EMPIRE

A.D. 476

A.D. 565

Byzantine Christianity

Although the Christian church was important in the west, it was central to the Byzantine Empire. Religion ruled every part of Byzantine society, according to historian Crane Brinton:

> At every important moment in the life of every person, the Church played an important role, governing marriage, and family relations, filling leisure time, helping to determine any critical decision. . . . The most serious intellectual problems . . . were those of theology, and they were attacked with zest by brains second to none in power. . . . The arts were largely . . . devoted to the representation of ecclesiastical [church] subjects. . . . Business was carried on under the auspices [support] of the Church.
>
> Religion also pervaded [filled] political life. . . . Issues, about which the people got excited, were political issues centering on theological problems. . . . It was not only in monasteries . . . that such problems were argued, but also in barber shops and among longshoremen on the docks. . . .
>
> Issues of foreign policy too were pervaded by religion: When the emperor went forth to war, he went as the champion of the faith.[59]

In the Byzantine Empire, unlike the western European kingdoms, no separation existed between church and state.

The emperor was the head of both. Historian Nicholas writes that he "summoned and presided over General [church] Councils and had to ratify their decrees. He appointed the patriarch of Constantinople [the highest bishop in the eastern church]. . . . Heresy [opinion or act contradictory to church teachings] was punished as a crime against the state."[60]

Religion went so deep in Byzantine society that in the first centuries of the Early Middle Ages, the two major political parties, the Blues and the Greens, represented not only different social classes but also different religious views. The Blues and the Greens were originally chariot racing teams, chariot racing being even more popular among the Byzantines than football, baseball, and basketball are in present-day United States.

The fans of the Blues tended to come from a different segment of Byzantine society than those of the Greens. Thus, the Blues fans came from the aristocracy, and the Greens from the lower class. These two social classes also represented the major political divisions in Constantinople, and eventually each group's association with its particular chariot-racing team turned sporting groups into political parties.

Although both parties were members of the eastern Christian church, the Blues held traditional beliefs, while the Greens generally did not. It was customary for an emperor to belong to either the Blues or the Greens, depending on how conventional his own beliefs were.

A lot of time and energy was spent in religious disputes, and much Byzantine writing consisted of long, complicated works about religious questions. All Byzantine citizens, from longshoremen to merchants to aristocrats, took part in these disputes. They argued religion with each other during work breaks, in barber shops, at mealtimes, in taverns, or in any other place where two or more Byzantines stopped to talk.

During the Early Middle Ages the Byzantines argued and fought, often physically and bloodily, over such issues as the relationship between Christ's human and divine nature and whether it was proper to worship painted or sculpted images of holy figures. These disputes often erupted into destructive riots that could last for days and sometimes could threaten even the safety of the emperor. These constant riots eventually weakened the Byzantine Empire.

Defender of Europe

The Byzantine Empire was one of the most important barriers standing between western Europe and a swarm of invaders during the Early Middle Ages. It was the Byzantines' successful defense of Constantinople against an Arab army in 717 that kept Muslim forces from invading eastern Europe.

During the Early Middle Ages the Byzantines also repelled Persian invasions, and they fought against various nomadic tribes that came out of central Asia. Although some invaders, such as the Bulgars, Avars, and Magyars, did conquer parts of eastern Europe, successful Byzantine resistance kept them from turning their full attention toward western Europe. Thus, the still struggling and young western kingdoms were provided with enough protection that they were not overrun.

The Byzantines were able to defend themselves so well because, during most of the Early Middle Ages, they had an excellent army and navy. Careful training supplemented strong, well-made steel swords, spears, and armor. The Byzantines had a signal corps that used mirrors to flash messages back and forth, an ambulance corps, and an efficient intelligence corps.

The Byzantine military was also adaptable. They adopted new tactics and new weapons from their enemies. They also had one of the first secret weapons in warfare, Greek fire. Although its exact nature is still unknown, Greek fire probably contained petroleum. It was pumped into bronze lion heads mounted on ships and then shot across the water to set enemy ships on fire. It was a fearsome weapon in the Early Middle Ages because it caught fire when exposed to air and, like all petroleum products, could not be put out with water. Its use helped clinch the Byzantine victory in the 717 Arab attack on Constantinople.

Byzantine Diplomacy

Although the Byzantine Empire had a good military, it preferred negotiations to war. Byzantine diplomatic missions were often successful, and the records show shrewd thinking and planning, accompanied by sharp bargaining.

Imperial agents kept track of affairs in all nearby states, providing money to any political factions that were friendly toward the Byzantine Empire. The Byzantine emperors often arranged for the sons of foreign leaders to be educated in Constantinople. When these young men returned to their homes, they brought with them a

The Byzantines had an excellent army (left) and navy. Adaptable, the Byzantine military adopted new tactics and weapons from enemies.

One of the weapons the Byzantines successfully adopted was Greek fire. Probably containing petroleum, Greek fire was pumped into bronze lion heads mounted on ships and shot across water to set enemy vessels on fire.

taste for Byzantine civilization. The emperors also arranged marriages between women of the Byzantine nobility and important local rulers. Sometimes an emperor would marry a non-Byzantine princess if he thought it the best way to create a bond between the empire and another state.

The Byzantine Economy

The Byzantine Empire's many wars and diplomatic efforts were expensive. However, despite the occasional financial crisis, the empire could afford them because, as the major trade center between Europe and Asia, it was rich. The imperial economy was so strong that the *nomisma*, the Byzantine gold piece, was the standard coin throughout the entire Mediterranean region for over eight hundred years, well into the Late Middle Ages.

At the heart of the Byzantine economy were very successful state-owned busi-

nesses and industries, such as farms, cattle ranches, gold and silver mines, and marble quarries. Also, the empire's treasure was helped by imperial monopolies on silk, purple dye, and gold embroidery, all important trade goods that were used for the ceremonial clothing of secular and religious leaders in both the east and the west. The rest of the empire's income came from taxes on everything from sales to property to inheritance.

Art and Learning in the Byzantine Empire

The wealth of the Byzantine Empire helped support an excellent school system and a dynamic arts scene, both of which gave the Byzantines a culture that was second to none during the Early Middle Ages. The imperial culture was quite different from that of the rough, developing lands of western Europe. Unlike the western em-

A Western Visitor in Constantinople

Western visitors to the Byzantine Empire were generally impressed by much of what they saw, particularly since the Byzantines had more advanced technical skills than their guests from the west. The following account by Bishop Liudprand from Cremona in northern Italy, quoted in The Eagle, the Crescent, and the Cross, *describes a visit in 950 to the court of the Byzantine emperor Constantine VII.*

"Before the emperor's seat stood a tree, made of bronze gilded over [covered with gold], whose branches were filled with birds, also made of gilded bronze, which uttered different cries, each according to its varying species. The throne itself was . . . of immense size and was guarded by lions, made either of bronze or of wood covered over with gold, who beat the ground with their tails and gave a dreadful roar with open mouth and quivering tongue. . . . After I had three times made obeisance [respect] to the emperor with my face upon the ground, I lifted my head and behold! the man whom just before I had seen sitting on a moderately elevated seat had now changed his raiment [clothes] and was sitting on the level of the ceiling. How it was done I could not imagine. . . . He [the emperor] did not address me directly . . . but by the intermediary [go-between] of a secretary. . . .

The emperor . . . invited me to dinner with him . . . . The emperor and his guests . . . recline on couches: and everything is served in vessels, not of silver, but of gold. . . . The solid fruit is brought on in . . . golden bowls, which are too heavy for men to lift. . . . Through openings in the ceiling hang three ropes . . . with golden rings. These rings are attached to the handles . . . [of] the bowls, and with four or five men helping from below, they [the bowls] are swung on to the table."

pire, the Byzantines still had most of their classical art and literature. Where learning was confined in the west almost exclusively to monasteries, in the east it was pursued in a large variety of secular schools, including the imperial university at Constantinople, and, according to Nicholas: "Primary education was available even in some smaller villages for both sexes: although formal higher education was normally restricted to men, many aristocratic women studied under tutors."[61] Byzantine teachers were important members of the society, and unlike in the west, the rulers of the empire, as well as other public figures, generally could read and write.

Where much classical Greek and Latin writing was lost in the west, most was saved in the Byzantine Empire, and Brinton writes that "had it not been for Byzantium, it seems certain that Plato and Aristotle, Homer and Sophocles would have been lost. We cannot even imagine what such a loss would have meant to western civilization."[62] In the Late Middle Ages Aristotle's work would become one of the major influences that shaped both secular and religious culture in western Europe, and all the ancient Greek and Roman writers were crucial in creating the culture of Renaissance Europe and, consequently, that of the modern world.

As original writers the Byzantines produced excellent histories but minor poetry. They also spent much energy on religious writings that were either complicated discussions about religious theory meant for the highly educated or simpler, more-dramatic retellings of the lives of the saints designed for the average reader.

Architecture was one of the great arts of the Byzantine Empire. The sixth-century Church of Santa Sophia combined the standard Roman public building, the basilica, which is shaped like a cross, with the dome that was popular in the Near East. The result was a new type of church of which the Byzantine historian Procopius said: "One feels at once that it is the work not of man's effort . . . , but . . . the work of the divine power; and the spirit . . . realizes that here God is very

The Byzantines were excellent at many of the arts, including architecture. The sixth-century church of Santa Sophia combined features of a Roman public building with the dome popular in the Near East.

near."[63] The design of Santa Sophia was quickly copied not only in other eastern churches, but also in western ones, and in 1453, when Constantinople fell to the Turks, these Muslim conquerors built their holy buildings along the same lines as Santa Sophia.

Besides architecture, the Byzantines were excellent at painting, mosaics, gold and silver working, and ivory carving. They produced elaborate silks and jeweled book covers, and their illustrated books were the models for the important western medieval art of illuminating manuscripts, practiced by western monks in both the Early and Late Middle Ages.

The Emperor Justinian I

The real glory of the Byzantine Empire began when Emperor Justinian I took the throne in 527. Justinian, who had had years of training under the previous emperor, his uncle Justin I, was not a Byzantine aristocrat. Indeed, the new emperor "was born . . . of lowly . . . peasants."[64] His origins may explain why as emperor, though he loved pomp and ceremony, he was also approachable, "for even men of low estate and altogether obscure had complete freedom not only to come before him but to converse with him."[65]

Upon becoming emperor, Justinian quickly swung into high gear. He immediately had the Byzantine laws studied in order to produce a unified, official version of the entire imperial legal code:

We [Justinian] have found the entire arrangement of the law which has come down to us from the foundation of the City of Rome . . . to be so con-

Emperor Justinian I was responsible for many of the achievements of the Byzantine Empire. He is perhaps best known for creating a unified imperial legal code.

fused that it is . . . not within the grasp of human capacity [understanding]. . . . We . . . begin by examining what had been enacted by former . . . princes, to correct their constitutions, and make them more easily understood. . . .

We have hastened to attempt the most complete and thorough amendment of the entire law, to collect and revise the whole body of Roman jurisprudence [law], and to assemble in one book the scattered treatises [writings] of so many authors; which no one else has heretofore [before] ventured to hope for or to expect, and it has indeed been . . . a most difficult

From the *Secret History* of Procopius

In his published writings, the Byzantine historian Procopius wrote glowingly about Justinian I, whom the scholar knew personally. However, in his Secret History, *quoted in Charles T. Davis's* The Eagle, the Crescent, and the Cross: Sources of Medieval History, *unpublished during his lifetime, the historian claimed that the emperor was the blackest of villains. To this day historians are still uncertain which account is more accurate.*

"[Justinian's] character was something I could not fully describe. For he was at once villainous and amenable [agreeable]; as people say . . . a moron. He was never truthful with anyone, but always guileful [deceitful] in what he said and did, yet easily hoodwinked by any who wanted to deceive him. His nature was an unnatural mixture of folly and wickedness. . . .

This Emperor . . . was deceitful, devious, false, . . . two-faced, cruel, . . . never moved to tears by either joy or pain, though he could summon them . . . at will when the occasion demanded, a liar always, not only offhand, but in writing, and when he swore sacred oaths to his subjects in their very hearing. Then he would immediately break his agreements and his pledges. . . . A faithless friend, he was a treacherous enemy, insane for murder and plunder, . . . easily led to anything evil, but never willing to listen to good counsel [advice], quick to plan mischief and carry it out, but finding even the hearing of anything good distasteful. . . .

Nature seemed to have taken the wickedness of all other men combined and planted it in this man's soul. . . . He was too prone to listen to accusations; and too quick to punish . . . , naming the punishment when he had heard only the accuser's side. . . . Without hesitation, he wrote decrees for the plundering of countries, sacking of cities, and slavery of whole nations, for no cause whatever. . . . I think it would be found that more men had been murdered by this single man than in all previous history."

undertaking, . . . one that was almost impossible.[66]

Out of Justinian's code would eventually grow most of the legal systems of modern Europe.

Justinian also launched an ambitious building project to replace certain public buildings burned in rioting. The emperor, however, did not want copies of the original buildings; he wanted something new, something better. Out of this desire on

Justinian's part came the great Church of Santa Sophia, which was just one sign of the vast cultural activity of the Byzantines under this ruler.

The Byzantine Empire reached its greatest extent under Justinian. Wanting to retake all the Roman territory lost in the previous century, the emperor appointed as general of the army the capable soldier Belisarius, who had won a spectacular victory against the empire's old enemy, the Persians. Belisarius quickly recaptured North Africa from the Vandals. Then, under Belisarius and later generals, the imperial army pushed the Ostrogoths out of Italy and retook the southern part of Spain from the Visigoths.

Belisarius appears before Justinian I with captive chieftains of the Vandals.

The Empress Theodora

Justinian was one of the most successful rulers of the entire Early Middle Ages. In part he owed his success to his own abilities, for, as historian Norman Cantor writes, "of all early medieval rulers Justinian was the best educated and possessed the greatest degree of native intelligence. . . . He was . . . the hardest-working man in the empire and greatly devoted to the state."[67]

However, Justinian's success was also due to his wife and empress, Theodora. Like her husband, Theodora was not a member of the aristocracy, her father having been a bear trainer, and she herself an actress and dancer, as well as, perhaps, a prostitute. This past did not prevent her from becoming the most powerful woman in the Early Middle Ages. Her husband, recognizing her abilities, made her coruler, with the same rights and powers he had.

Because Justinian belonged to the Blues and Theodora to the Greens, the two often found themselves working toward different ends. Historian Will Durant writes: "She took an active part in diplomacy and in . . . [church] politics. . . . Sometimes she countermanded [canceled] her husband's orders, often to the advantage of the state." But, no matter how difficult Theodora's plotting made Justinian's work, the emperor "bore with . . . patience her interferences with his schemes."[68]

At one time Anthemius, the patriarch of Constantinople, refused to obey Justinian. The emperor exiled the patriarch from the city, but the empress, feeling that the sentence was unjust, hid Anthemius in her apartment for two years while she

Justinian's wife and empress, Theodora, was a remarkable woman. Knowledgeable and shrewd, Theodora ruled alongside Justinian and was largely responsible for keeping Justinian in power.

tried to have the exile canceled. Failing in her efforts, Theodora sent Anthemius into exile, but just barely. She installed him in her palace across the Bosporus, which was only two miles from Constantinople.

It was Theodora who saved Justinian during the greatest crisis of his emperorship, the Nika revolt of 532. During a rare moment of cooperation between the Blues and Greens, Justinian managed to anger both parties, thus setting off rioting. Tens of thousands of people rampaged through the city streets, killing police and other government officials and burning down many public buildings. The name *Nika* comes from the Greek word for victory that rioters yelled as they swarmed through the streets of Constantinople.

According to historian Procopius only Theodora's shaming of Justinian kept him from fleeing the city and thus losing his throne:

> My [Theodora's] opinion is that now . . . is a bad time to flee, even if this should bring safety. . . . For a man who has been an Emperor to become a refugee is not to be borne. May I never be separated from the purple [the imperial color] and may I no longer live on that day when those who meet me shall not call me mistress. Now if you wish to save yourself, O Emperor, this is not hard. For we have much money; there is the sea, here are the boats. But think whether after you have been saved you may not come to feel that you would have preferred to die. As for me, I like a certain old proverb that says: royalty is a good shroud [burial garment].[69]

Justinian stayed, and after Belisarius put down the revolt (killing some thirty thousand people in the process), the emperor ruled for another thirty-three years.

The Slavs

At about the time that Justinian became emperor, the Byzantine Empire's northern border, the Danube River, was being crossed by raiders from a new group of barbarians, the Slavs. The Slavs came from an area that stretched over what is now eastern Poland and the western Ukraine.

They began moving into eastern and central Europe when the German tribes moved west and south. During most of the sixth century they raided the northern Balkan provinces of the empire.

In the seventh century the Byzantines made a rare but costly diplomatic mistake. They arranged for the Avars, a people related to the Huns, to attack the Slavs. The empire hoped that this attack would keep the Slavs too busy fighting the Avars to have time for raiding the Balkans.

The plan misfired badly, as large armies of Slavs, fleeing the Avars, drove deep into the Balkans, occasionally threatening Constantinople itself. Many of the Slavs ended up staying and occupying the Balkan peninsula.

Further, the Avars soon turned on the Byzantines and began attacking the Balkans with armies composed of conquered Slavs. Historian A.P. Vlasto notes that the Byzantines could see "in retrospect that to allow the militaristic . . . Avars to manipulate the Slavs, who were potentially sedentary settlers and valuable as such, was . . . [a] mistake."[70]

Two of the early Slavic kingdoms founded in the Balkans were Serbia and Croatia. Although neighbors, they were politically and religiously divided because the Serbs eventually became members of the eastern Christian church and the Croats of the western.

The conversion of the Slavs was divided fairly equally between the Roman and Byzantine churches, each normally winning over those groups of Slavs closest to it. Thus, the eastern church pulled in Slavs living in the central and eastern Balkans and Russia, while the western church took in Slavs in central Europe and the northwestern Balkans. One Byzantine missionary, Cyril, played an important role in the development of Slavic culture when he created the Cyrillic alphabet that is still used today in Russia and other parts of Eastern Europe.

Persians and Muslims

Upon Justinian's death in 565, the Byzantine Empire was the largest, most powerful state in Europe. However, the empire's populace, particularly in the conquered territories of Africa, Italy, and Spain, were angry over harsh laws designed to suppress any religious views that did not agree with Justinian's. Also, the imperial treasury that had been full when Justinian became emperor was now empty because of the costs of his foreign wars. To pay for the governing of the conquered lands, taxes were high, made even higher by corrupt tax collectors.

Justinian's conquests cost the empire more than just money. Because the Byzantines had to shift soldiers and material to Africa, Italy, and Spain, they weakened their border defenses and, as a result, lost the northern Balkans to the Slavs. The empire's weakened eastern border led to attacks by the Persian Empire, which grabbed off large chunks of the Byzantine state, including Egypt. For a time, the empire appeared doomed.

In 610, when Byzantine fortunes were at their lowest, Heraclius, son of the governor of Africa, seized the imperial throne. It took the new emperor ten hard years to rebuild "the morale of the people, the strength of the army, and the resources of the treasury," according to Will Durant.[71] Then Heraclius set out and defeated the

Persians and regained all the territory lost to them, even though he ended up having to fight not only the Persians but also the Avars, who laid siege to Constantinople while the Persians threatened the city from across the Bosporus.

However, Heraclius's victory was costly. Both the Byzantine Empire and the Per-

---

Conversion of the Russians

Although not as active in sending missionaries out as the Roman church, the Byzantine church still played an important role in converting Europe to Christianity. Indeed, at the end of the Early Middle Ages, it was the eastern church, not the western, that won the following of the Russians. The twelfth-century Russian Primary Chronicle *describes the conversion of Prince Vladimir of Kiev in 988, as quoted in* The Eagle, the Crescent, and the Cross.

"Then came the Germans, asserting that they were come as emissaries of the Pope. . . . Vladimir inquired what their teaching was. They replied, 'Fasting according to one's strength. But whatever one eats or drinks is all to the glory of God.' . . . Then Vladimir answered, 'Depart hence; our fathers accepted no such principle.' . . .

Then the Greeks [Byzantines] sent to Vladimir a scholar. . . . He exhibited to Vladimir a canvas on which was depicted the Judgment Day of the Lord, and showed him, on the right, the righteous going to . . . Paradise, and on the left, the sinners on their way to torment. Then Vladimir sighed and said, 'Happy are they upon the right, but woe to those upon the left!' The scholar replied, 'If you desire to take your place upon the right with the just, then accept baptism!' . . .

Vladimir summoned together his boyars [nobles] and the city-elders [of Kiev], and . . . they chose good and wise men to . . . go . . . among the Germans, and examine their faith, and finally to visit the Greeks. . . .

The [Byzantine] Emperor sent a message . . . to prepare the church and the clergy. . . . The Emperor accompanied the Russes [Russians] to the church . . . , calling their attention to the beauty of the edifice [building], the chanting, and the . . . services . . . and dismissed them with valuable presents and great honor.

Thus, they returned to their own country. . . . The envoys reported, . . . 'We went to . . . the Greeks . . . , and their service is fairer than the ceremonies of other nations.' . . . Vladimir then inquired where they should all accept baptism."

Although Heraclius defeated the Persians and the Avars to defend the Byzantine Empire, he so severely weakened the state as a result that Muslim armies captured all Byzantine holdings outside the Balkans.

sians were drained by the years of war, and they were easy marks for the Muslim armies that burst out of Arabia in 634. As the Arabs swept over the Near East and then across Africa and into Spain, Persia fell to them, as did much of the Byzantine Empire. By the middle of the eighth century, almost all of the empire's land outside of the Balkans was gone.

Bulgars and Iconoclasts

Even the remaining Balkan provinces were not secure from attack, as an aggressive group of Asian nomads, the Bulgars, hit the empire hard from the north. In 811 these new invaders destroyed an imperial army that was, in turn, invading the Bulgar regions and killed Emperor Nicephorus I. He was the first emperor to die in battle in four and a half centuries. Two years later the Bulgars hit Constantinople, burning the city's suburbs. Eventually the Bulgars began coming under Byzantine influence when they converted to Christianity, although it required more than a century of on-again, off-again war to complete the job begun by that conversion.

While the Bulgars threatened from the north, imperial officials, from the emperor on down, as well as ordinary citizens, focused their attention on the latest religious controversy, Iconoclasm, which means destroying religious images. This movement, which began in the imperial provinces of Asia Minor, claimed that holy statues and painted images, or icons, of the Virgin Mary, Christ, and the various saints found in Byzantine churches, monasteries, shops, and houses were sinful. The Iconoclasts were particularly upset because people seemed to worship the icons, a practice that smacked of the classical religions of Rome and Greece. Author Harry J. Magoulias states that the image breakers also "took their stand on the second commandment: 'Thou shalt not make unto thee any graven image [object of worship]'. . . . From the New Testament [the Iconoclasts'] chief text was: 'God is a spirit: and they that worship him must worship him in spirit.'"[72]

In 726 the Byzantine emperor Leo III forbade the use and display of icons. Riots exploded as soldiers removing icons were attacked by angry citizens. Civil war erupted when rebels in favor of icons declared their

Iconoclasts destroy holy images. Iconoclasts believed that icons depicting the saints and other holy figures were sacrilegious. Several Byzantine emperors were Iconoclasts.

independence from Constantinople. Later the rebel cause was sunk, along with its fleet, by the imperial navy.

In the west, Pope Gregory II condemned Iconoclasm and Leo's policies. Leo struck back by removing southern Italy from the pope's authority. The loss of this territory damaged the papacy's prestige and cost its treasury the rents from church-owned land in the area.

The next two emperors were also Iconoclasts, with Leo's son, Constantine V, being a particularly brutal enforcer of Iconoclasm. Constantine had thousands of icons destroyed and had their supporters tortured, mutilated, and killed. Iconoclasm was finally outlawed in 843, sixty-eight years after Constantine's death. But even during those years it played only a minor role in imperial politics.

The Macedonians

In the last part of the ninth century, a new line of emperors, the Macedonians, came to power. They ruled through the remainder of the Early Middle Ages and proved to be popular with the Byzantine people, partially because they won back some of the land that had been lost to the Arabs.

The first Macedonian emperor was Basil I, who, like Justinian I, had been born a peasant. After spending much of his early life as a Bulgar slave, Basil escaped and reached Constantinople when he was twenty-five. In the capital Basil's cleverness and lack of principles enabled him to rise quickly. Beginning as a diplomat's groom, he eventually became coemperor with Michael III, whom Basil finally assassinated to become sole emperor in 867.

Despite such ruthlessness, Basil I and the later Macedonian emperors proved to be good for the Byzantine Empire. By the end of the Early Middle Ages, the Byzantine state had once more reached "the power, wealth, and culture of its zenith [height] under Justinian. Asia Minor [and other areas] . . . had been wrested [taken] from the Moslems . . . ; the Balkans had been recaptured from Bulgars and Slavs," reports Will Durant.[73] Constantinople had more trade, more wealth, and more art than Rome had at its height.

Trouble for the empire, however, lay ahead. During Macedonian rule a new political group arose in the empire. This group was made up of noble landowners, many of whom had built up huge estates, often by virtual theft of others' land. These landlords and the emperors were soon locked in a struggle for control of the Byzantine state. In the late tenth century Emperor Basil II passed laws that hit hard at the powerful nobles, breaking up a number of the largest estates. However, after Basil II's death, the landowners managed to have these laws repealed, leaving no brake on the growth of their estates or their power. The unchecked landowners would lead the Byzantine Empire into disaster during the Late Middle Ages.

Chapter

6 The New Religion: Islam and Southern Europe

At the end of the Byzantine Empire's seventh-century war with Persia, Justinian's dream of reviving the old Roman Empire seemed back on track. The Byzantines had regained all their provinces lost to the Persians. But, then, a new enemy struck and within a century had swept away most of the imperial land outside of the Balkans. These former imperial lands were now in the hands of the Arabs, who were newly converted to Islam, the religion founded by the prophet Muhammad.

Islam (Arabic for "surrendering to the will of God") was to become one of the world's great religions. Its followers, known as Muslims (Arabic for "those who surrender"), would conquer the Near East, North Africa, and Spain before their holy war was over (they would also eventually spread east through Asia, finally reaching the Philippines).

During the Early Middle Ages, the contact between Muslims and European Christians was frequently violent, as in the Muslim conquest of Spain, their invasion of Sicily and southern Italy, their occasional battles with the Franks, and their on-again, off-again war with the Byzantines. However, the civilization that would grow in the Muslim world, particularly that in Spain, would be crucial to the development of western Europe in the Late Middle Ages.

Muhammad, founder and prophet of Islam, with the two symbols of his faith, the sword and the Koran. The holy city of Mecca is in the background.

Muhammad

Muhammad (Arabic for "highly praised") was the prophet and founder of Islam. Born in the Arabian trading city of Mecca

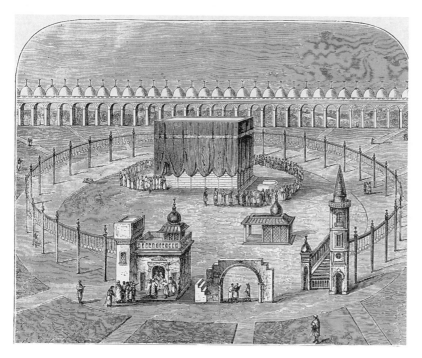

The Arabs worshiped deities in the stars and the moon and sacred stones. The most important of these stones was said to have fallen from heaven. It was kept in the Kaaba (pictured) in the holy city of Mecca.

around 570, he became a trader before marrying a wealthy widow. After his marriage Muhammad had the time and the money to pursue his growing interest in religion, and he began learning more about various religions, such as Christianity and Judaism.

Muhammad often spent nights alone, meditating in a nearby mountain cave. On one such night his interest in religion became a mission when in 610 he had a vision of the angel Gabriel, as quoted by historian Will Durant:

> Whilst I [Muhammad] was asleep, with a coverlet of silk brocade [upon which] was some writing, the angel Gabriel appeared to me and said, "Read!" I said, "I do not read." He pressed me with the coverlets so tightly that methought 'twas death. Then he let me go, and said, "Read!" . . . So I read aloud, and he departed from me

at last. And I awoke from my sleep, and it was as though these words were written on my heart. I went forth until . . . I heard a voice from heaven saying, "O Mohammed [Muhammad]! thou art the messenger of Allah [God] and I am Gabriel." I raised my head toward heaven to see, and lo, [there was] Gabriel in the form of a man, with feet set evenly on the rim of the sky.[74]

Muhammad began preaching, explaining this and other revelations that came to him in visions.

The Arabs to whom he preached had a number of gods, according to Durant: "The desert Arab . . . worshiped . . . deities in stars and moon and the depths of the earth. . . . Here and there he worshiped sacred stones."[75] The most important of these stones, the Black Stone, was in Mecca in the Kaaba (Arabic for "cubic building"), along with several idols. The

A page from a thirteenth-century Koran, the holy book of Islam. The Koran, a collection of Muslim teachings, was first produced after Muhammad's death.

Black Stone, an oval some seven inches in diameter, was said to have fallen from heaven and was probably a meteorite.

Muhammad's teachings called for rejection of these Arabic gods and for belief in a single God, Allah, who was the same as that worshiped by Jews and Christians. Muhammad felt that the beliefs of both Judaism and Christianity were generally true but that both earlier religions were incomplete and that his visions from God contained the final truth.

Muhammad's preachings were not accepted in Mecca, so in 622 he went to another Arabian city, Yathrib, which became the center for the new religion and which changed its name to al-Medina, meaning "the" city. Muhammad's move to al-Medina, or Medina, became known as the Hegira (Arabic for "flight"), and the year 622 became the year 1 of the Muslim calendar.

Ten years later Muhammad and his followers from Medina attacked and took Mecca. The idols in the Kaaba were destroyed, although the Black Stone was kept and became an important holy object for Muslims. By the time of Muhammad's death in 632, a third of the Arabs had accepted Islam and become members of an Islamic state, and by a century after his death, Islamic states controlled the Near East, North Africa, and Spain.

The Beliefs of Islam

After Muhammad's death Islam began to take a more formal shape. Muhammad's teachings were collected in the Koran, the Islamic holy book. Because the teachings were arranged by length, the longest coming first, rather than by subject matter, and because Muhammad often used made-up names for people and places, the Koran is difficult to understand. This diffi-

The Constitution of Medina

Unable to win support in his home city of Mecca, Muhammad went to Medina in 622, where he established a religious government and set down rules of conduct for Muslims. These rules became known as the Constitution of Medina, which was the first official document of Islam. This excerpt is from Medieval Europe: A Short Sourcebook.

"In the name of God the Compassionate, the Merciful. This is a document from [Muhammad] the prophet. . . .

The God-fearing believers shall be against the rebellious or him who seeks to spread injustice, or sin . . . , or corruption between believers; the hand of every man shall be against him even if he be a son of one of them . . . . Believers are friends one to the other to the exclusion of outsiders. To the Jew who follows us belong help and equality. He shall not be wronged nor shall his enemies be aided. . . . The believers must avenge the blood of one another shed in the way of God. The God-fearing believers enjoy the best and most upright guidance. . . . Whoever is convicted of killing a believer without good reason shall be subject to retaliation unless the next of kin is satisfied with [blood money]. . . .

It shall not be lawful to a believer who holds by what is in this document and believes in God and the last [judgment] day to help an evil-doer . . . or to shelter him. The curse of God and His anger on the day of resurrection [judgment day] will be upon him if he does. . . . Whenever you differ about a matter it must be referred to God and to [Muhammad]. . . .

God approves of this document. This deed [writing] will not protect the unjust and the sinner. The man who goes forth to fight and the man who stays at home . . . is safe unless he had been unjust and sinned. God is the protector of the good and God-fearing man and [Muhammad] is the prophet of God."

culty has produced a whole body of writings to explain the book's meaning.

Basic to the belief of all Muslims are the five duties, or the Pillars of Islam. The first duty is to confirm one's faith by saying publicly that "there is no god but Allah, and Muhammad is his prophet." The second duty requires five daily prayers made in the direction of the Kaaba in Mecca. The third duty is to give alms, or money, to the poor. The fourth is to fast from sunrise to sunset each day of the holy month of Ramadan (the ninth month of the Islamic year). The final duty of the Muslim is to make a pilgrimage to the Kaaba in Mecca.

Jihad and Expansion

Islam continued to expand rapidly in the years after Muhammad's death, with much of that expansion coming in a war that began in 634. The Arabs called this and similar holy wars a jihad, which is Arabic for "battle".

Despite its Arabic definition, a jihad does not have to be a war, although certainly the one that began in 634 was. Even when a jihad is a war, its stated purpose is not to grab territory or to force nonbelievers to convert. Rather, it is to seize political power in order to reach Islam's goal of changing the earth. This seizure can be done through any number of ways, war being only one of them.

The Byzantine Empire, the first European state to feel the impact of the Islamic jihad, lost Egypt, Syria, and Palestine, including Jerusalem, within five years to the Arabs. North Africa followed sixty years later, and the Visigothic kingdom of Spain was snuffed out in the early eighth century by a Muslim army from Tangiers. Later, Arabs would conquer Sicily and various other Mediterranean islands. Sicily would be used as a base to land troops in southern Italy, from which the Muslims would threaten Rome and the papacy through the last part of the Early Middle Ages.

However, the Muslims were not unbeatable, and though they tried twice to take the city of Constantinople, thus opening up a route into eastern Europe, they failed both times. Another northward thrust was stopped at Tours by the Franks. By the end of the Early Middle Ages, the Muslim states were no longer as strong as

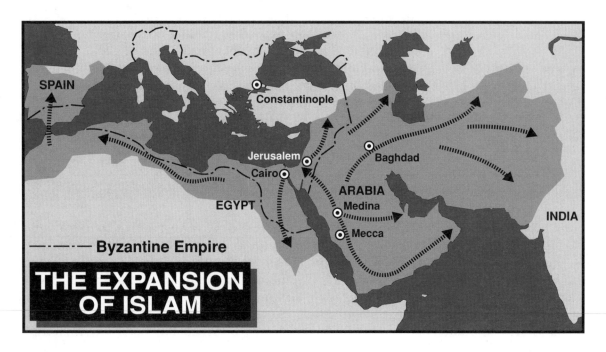

THE EXPANSION OF ISLAM

The Muslim Conquest of Spain

Spain, conquered by the Muslims in the eighth century, became one of the great centers of Muslim culture. As such, it played an important role in the development of the Western world, beginning in the Late Middle Ages. The ninth-century Egyptian Ibn Abd-el-Hakem detailed the Muslim conquest in his History of the Conquest of Spain, *quoted in Charles T. Davis's* The Eagle, the Crescent, and the Cross. *As with most medieval historians, whether Christian or Muslim, the Egyptian writer did not attempt to separate fact from fiction.*

"The news of Tarik [leader of the Muslims] . . . reached the people of Andalus [Spain]. Tarik, . . . having passed by an island in the sea, . . . left behind . . . a division of his troops. . . . The Moslems . . . . found no other inhabitants there, than vinedressers [ones who raise grape vines]. . . . They took one of the vinedressers, . . . cut him in pieces, and boiled him. . . . They had also boiled [animal] meat. . . . When the meat was cooked, they threw away the flesh of the man . . . , no one knowing that it was thrown away: and they ate the meat. . . . [The vinedressers] . . . informed the people of Andalus that the Moslems feed on human flesh. . . .

There was a house in Andalus, the door of which was secured with padlocks, and on which every new king of the country placed a padlock . . . , until . . . the king against whom the Moslems marched . . . refused [to place a padlock] saying, I will place nothing . . . , until I know what is inside; he then ordered it to be opened; . . . inside were portraits of the Arabs, and a letter . . . , 'When this door shall be opened, these people will invade this country.' . . .

When Tarik landed, soldiers from Cordova [a Spanish city] came to meet him; and seeing the small number of his companions they despised him. . . . The battle with Tarik was severe. [The Spanish soldiers] were routed. . . . When [Spain's king] Roderic heard of this, he came to their rescue. . . . [The Muslims and the Spanish] fought a severe battle; but God, mighty and great, killed Roderic and his companions."

they had been, and the Byzantine Empire was able to recapture some of its lost territory, although most of it was gone forever, remaining Muslim to this day.

As with most human undertakings, the growth of Islam was not driven strictly by ideals. It was also fueled by a need to relieve the overpopulation of seventh-century Arabia. Even before the jihad, many Arabs had moved into neighboring Syria, Iraq, and Palestine. The jihad merely speeded up this process. (In later centuries medieval Muslim rulers would often use jihads as excuses to expand their territories.)

The 634 jihad's success was helped greatly by both the Byzantine and Persian Empires being drained by years of fighting one another. Additionally, the Byzantine emperor Heraclius, having recently returned Egypt and Syria to his empire, had cracked down on Jews and on Christian heretics, who made up the bulk of the population of these imperial provinces, and who welcomed the arrival of the Arabs as an escape from Heraclius's policy.

The Arabs' cause was often helped because they did not oppress Christians and Jews, who like the Muslim Arabs believed in a single God and who were "peoples of the Book," although it was the Bible and not the Koran. The Arabs' broad-mindedness did serve Muslim self-interest, for Islamic states placed a "tax and limitation of political rights on those who would not recognize [Muhammad] as the Prophet of Allah, and therefore they had a vested interest in not hurrying the conversion of their subjects," according to historian Norman Cantor.[76]

Sunnites and Shiites

For a period after the death of Muhammad, the new Islamic state was ruled by a single leader, known as the caliph (from Arabic, meaning "representative"—in this case, of Muhammad). However, this post became the prize in a civil war that broke out in 656 between the two major groups of Muslims, the Shiites and the Sunnites. The Shiites wanted a member of Muhammad's family to be caliph, while the Sun-

nites desired to elect any Muslim capable of handling the job. The Shiites also believed that the Koran needed no written explanations and should stand alone, while the Sunnites felt that the book required additional writings to make its teachings clear.

The Shiite-Sunnite civil war resulted in the Islamic state's breaking into separate units, some, such as Egypt, governed by Shiites, and others, such as Spain, by Sunnites. Generally, says Cantor, "the rulers of these states continued to respect the caliph as the successor of the Prophet, but the political power in the Islamic world had now fallen into the hands of various . . . princes."[77] Meanwhile, the caliphate [office of a caliph] passed through first Sunnite hands and then into Shiite hands. The Shiites moved the caliphate to Baghdad in Iraq, which was a Shiite stronghold.

The New Culture

The culture of the Muslim world during the Early Middle Ages was far more advanced than that found in most of Europe. As historian Philip K. Hitti observes: "While [caliphs] al-Rashid and al-Mamun were . . . [reading] Greek and Persian philosophy . . . Charlemagne and his lords . . . were . . . dabbling in [playing with] the art of writing their names."[78] The only European state to have a culture that rivaled the Islamic states was the Byzantine Empire.

The richness of the Islamic culture during the Early Middle Ages resulted in part from the cultural gains that came with the conquest of Egypt and Persia, homes of very old civilizations. It also developed from the sharing of ideas between people brought together from all parts of the Muslim world by the pilgrimage to Mecca. Also, some parts of the culture, such as literature, were spurred on, according to Crane Brinton, because Arabic

> had to be learned by everybody who wished to read the Koran, since it was the rule that the Book might not be translated. . . . [Muslims] felt that incessant study of it [Arabic] was necessary . . . , and they gave the highest position among the arts to the composing of poetry.[79]

Finally, the Muslim culture may have benefited from a tradition that said that Muhammad himself had urged his followers to learn, saying that "he who leaves his home in search of knowledge walks in the path of God."[80]

Muslims in the Early Middle Ages also became interested in science. The ninth-century caliph Mamun built observatories and had the works of Greek scientists translated into Arabic. He even tried unsuccessfully to get a famous Byzantine mathematician to come to Baghdad. The caliph's efforts created an interest in mathematics and science among Byzantine officials, subjects to which they had formerly paid little attention.

Mathematics and Medicine

It was Muslim mathematicians who introduced Europe to the concept of zero and to Arabic numerals, both of which the Arabs brought from India. Both of these Muslim mathematical tools would lead to the growth of modern science that began

Muslim culture during the Early Middle Ages was far more advanced than its European counterparts. In the ninth century, the Muslims had built observatories where astronomers studied the stars and planets.

with Galileo in the Renaissance and make possible today's higher mathematics and complex calculations.

The Muslims also excelled at medicine, their medical books providing the most accurate and thorough descriptions of the symptoms and course of smallpox, measles, and eye disease to be found until the eighteenth century. Their doctors had to pass tests in order to practice. Will Durant writes that Islamic scientists were among the first real chemists, introducing "precise observation, controlled experiment, and careful records. They . . . chemically analyzed . . . substances, . . . studied and manufactured hundreds of drugs."[81]

Muslim Spain

The Muslim state of Cordova in Spain became one of the great centers of learning in both the Muslim and Christian worlds. According to historian J. W. Draper:

> Scarcely had the Arabs become firmly settled in Spain when. . . . they established libraries in all their chief towns; it is said that not fewer than seventy were in existence. To every mosque [Muslim place of worship] was attached a public school, in which the children of the poor were taught to read and write. . . . For the [rich] . . . there were academies. . . . In Cordova, . . . there were universities. . . . In the universities, some of the professors . . . gave lectures on Arabic classical works; others taught . . . composition, or mathematics, or astronomy. . . . From these institutions many of the practices observed in our [modern] colleges were derived. . . . They had also, in addition to these schools of general learning, professional ones, particularly in medicine.[82]

In Cordova western Europeans would later find Arabic translations of Greek

The Muslim state of Cordova in Spain became one of the great centers of learning. Pictured is the interior of an ancient Cordovan mosque built in the eighth century.

works no longer available in the west. They used these texts to help build the civilizations of the Late Middle Ages and the Renaissance. By the middle of the ninth century, many Spanish Christians were finding Islamic culture more to their liking than their own, as this Spanish writer of the times complained:

> My fellow-Christians delight in the poems and romances of the Arabs; they study the works of [Muslim] . . . philosophers, not in order to refute them, but to acquire a correct and elegant Arabic style. Where today can a layman [nonprofessional] be found, who reads the Latin Commentaries on the Holy Scriptures? Who is there that studies the Gospels, the Prophets, the Apostles? Alas! The young Christians who are most conspicuous for their talents have no knowledge of any literature or language save the Arabic; they read and study Arabic books with avidity [eagerness], they amass whole libraries of them at immense cost, and they everywhere sing the praises of Arabic lore [knowledge].[83]

The Arabic poems referred to in the quotation were love poetry, which were the models for songs and poems about love in the Late Middle Ages. The Muslim culture also gave to the Europeans of the Late Middle Ages, and to the later Western world, such architectural features as pointed arches and the stone patterning called arabesque. It also gave the West such musical instruments as the tambourine, the guitar, and the lute. In numerous other ways as well, both in peace and war, Muslim culture would be a major influence on the development of European civilization in the coming Late Middle Ages.

7 The Last of the Barbarians: The Vikings

During the ninth and tenth centuries—the last two of the Early Middle Ages—seafaring Vikings, fierce warriors from the Scandinavian north, attacked and looted Europe from England to Constantinople. These Vikings were feared by all who had contact with them, and, according to historian Crane Brinton,

> the invasions of the . . . Vikings proved to be a severe blow for western Europe. For France, the Low Countries, and the British Isles, the ninth and tenth centuries were in some respects the low point, the period of greatest disintegration and darkness.[84]

The Norse

The Scandinavians, known as Northmen or Norse, were descended from German tribes that had moved into the region of Denmark, Norway, and Sweden, and thus, they were the last of the people labeled barbarians by the Romans to trouble Europe. At the time the Viking raids began, the Norse were still practicing a form of the old German religion and still worshiping the old gods, such as Odin and Thor. The harsh winter climate of Scandinavia colored this religion: to these northern-

ers, hell was a place of ice and bitter cold, not fire and blistering heat as with the Christians.

The Norse had few villages. Rather, most of them lived on isolated farms that had one large house in which everyone—family, workers, and slaves—stayed. In addition to farming, hunting and fishing were also major sources of food. Unlike the earlier German tribes, the Norse did not limit any of this work to a particular group, such as women or slaves. All classes—nobles and peasants, men and women—worked, and "nearly every Northman was a craftsman, especially skilled in wood."[85]

Like other Germans, the Norse had a warrior aristocracy. The tenth-century Muslim diplomat Ibn Fadlan left one of the best descriptions of these Norse warriors and their women, whom he met near the Volga River:

> Never had I seen a people of more perfect physique. . . . They wear neither coat or *kaftan* [robe], but each man carried a cape which covers one half of his body, leaving one hand free. No one is ever parted from his axe, sword, and knife. Their swords are Frankish in design, broad, flat, and fluted [grooved]. Each man has a

number of trees, figures, and the like [tattooed] from the finger-nails to the neck. Each woman carries on her bosom a container made of iron, silver, copper, or gold—its size and substance depending on her man's wealth. Attached to the container is a ring carrying her knife. . . . Round her neck she wears gold or silver rings: when a man collects 10,000 dirhams [Muslim silver coins] he gives his wife a neck-ring, when he has 20,000 he gives two rings. . . . One woman often has many neck-rings.[86]

Although Norse society was dominated by the men, women had rights and privileges. Marriages among the Norse were arranged by parents, but a woman had the right to refuse a proposed husband. Husbands were expected to seek and seriously consider their wives' advice about business, and wives shared in their husbands' wealth, one-third at marriage, rising to one-half at the end of twenty years.

Upper-class Norse families were large because the men often had more than one wife. Large families, however, created a problem. The more sons each family had, the less each son got for his inheritance. This male overpopulation may have caused some Norse warriors to become Vikings in order to find ways of increasing their wealth. Others became Vikings because they had been exiled from their northern homes, while many simply were drawn by adventure.

The Raids

The first Viking raids were small affairs, involving only a handful of ships. The raiders would attack a coastal village or monastery and then return home with some loot, as well as a few slaves. However, as understanding of what the lands south of them offered, the Vikings began assembling fleets of ships so they could mount

Norse ships allowed the Vikings to attack swiftly and efficiently. Powered by both oars and sails, the ships were extremely manageable and could sail the oceans as well as along rivers.

Viking raids were extremely successful. The Vikings approached their victims by sea, giving the inhabitants little or no warning. The Vikings swarmed over the land, took what they wanted, and quickly sailed home.

attacks against larger and richer targets, such as London or Paris. Eventually the northern raiders grabbed land and built permanent bases from which to conduct their raids.

The Vikings' ships gave the northerners a great advantage in the type of hit-and-run raids they liked. Small and powered by both sails and oars, these ships were very manageable and could readily sail up rivers, such as the Thames in Britain or the Seine in the western Frankish kingdom, according to David Nicholas: "The geography of northwestern Europe, laced with streams that were easily navigable by the small Viking keels [of their ships], . . . made the region an easy prey for naval attacks."[87]

The Vikings' water approach gave their victims little or no warning. In raids from the sea the Norse sailed right up to a beach, whereas with river attacks, they sailed to the mouth of a river and then quickly rowed up to reach their goal. In both types of raids, once the Vikings reached the shore, they swarmed out, generally meeting little resistance, and took what they wanted. The raid finished, the Vikings shoved off and were long gone before land forces, slowed by bad roads—or no roads at all—could reach them. Other ships were rarely a threat to them, because they were slower and less maneuverable than those of the Vikings.

The Viking Reputation

The Norse frightened those they attacked. The northerners seemed without fear and also without pity or mercy. They were savage in their raids—killing, looting, and burning—and left little behind them. Since they were not Christians, they did not hesitate to kill priests and monks and loot and burn churches and monasteries. To Christian Europe, Vikings seemed like devils released from hell.

Records from the time of the attacks note the regular appearance of the northern raiders with the same inevitability as the coming of winter, as can be seen in these 848 and 849 entries from a Frankish history: "the heathen [the Vikings], as was their custom, inflicted injury on the Christians" and "the heathen from the North wrought havoc [created destruction] in Christendom as usual and grew greater in strength."[88]

These Viking raids had a major effect on western European life. They strengthened the feudal system at the expense of central authority. In response to the continuing onslaughts, warlords built castles and fortresses where people could hide safely during a Norse raid. Thus, the lords of these castles became more important to the local people than any king or emperor who was too far away to be of help.

Alfred the Great and the Danelaw

According to the *Anglo-Saxon Chronicle*, the first recorded Viking raid hit Britain in 787 when "came three ships to the West Saxon shores . . . and they slew [killed] folk."[89] These raiders were from Denmark, as would be the majority of other Vikings to attack the British kingdoms. In 865, less than a century later, the Danes had moved in, establishing settlements of their own in the center of Britain. From these permanent bases they mounted constant attacks against the Saxon kingdoms in southern Britain, and within ten years only the Saxon kingdom of Wessex was not under their control.

In 871 Aethelred, the king of Wessex, was killed fighting the Danes and was succeeded by Alfred, his younger brother. Alfred immediately attacked the Danes, but he was so badly beaten that he had to pay the Vikings in order to save his kingdom.

Alfred the Great, king of Wessex, reorganized the army, established a common law, rebuilt cities, and accomplished other feats that made him well loved among his people.

In 878 the young Saxon king again fought and lost to a Danish army, but later that same year he defeated the northerners at the Battle of Ethandun (now Edington).

Alfred was not strong enough to force the Danes out of Britain, but with the Peace of Wedmore, he was able to draw new boundary lines between his kingdom and their holdings. Thus, Alfred ruled over southern and west central Britain, while the Danes had the north, including Scotland, and the east central regions. This Danish section became known as the Danelaw.

Partially because of his victory, the Saxon king became known in the histories as Alfred the Great. However, this title also recognized his other deeds while king of Wessex, as detailed by historian Will Durant:

Like . . . Charlemagne, he [Alfred] turned to the work of . . . government. He reorganized the army, built a navy, established a common law . . . , reformed the administration of justice, provided legal protection for the poor, built or rebuilt cities and towns, and erected "royal halls . . . with wood and stone" for his growing governmental staff. An eighth of his revenue [income] was devoted to relief of the poor; another eighth to education. At Reading, his capital, he established a palace school, and gave abundantly to the educational . . . work of churches and monasteries. . . . He sent abroad for scholars . . . to come and instruct his people and himself. . . . Recognizing, almost before any other European, the rising importance of the

A young Alfred the Great leads his troops against the Danes. Although he did not successfully defeat the Danes, Alfred was able to establish separate territories between them and his own kingdom.

Alfred the Great on Education

Like Charlemagne, the Saxon king Alfred the Great, late ninth-century ruler of southern Britain, was enthusiastic about education. Alfred had a number of books translated from Latin into Saxon, his native language, so that his fellow Britons might more easily read them. In his preface to the translation of Pope Gregory I's The Book of the Pastoral Rule, *as quoted in* A Source Book of Medieval History, *the Saxon king describes the sorry state of education in ninth-century Britain and proposes an educational plan.*

"It has often come into my mind what wise men there formerly were throughout England [Britain] . . . ; and how foreigners came to this land in search of wisdom and instruction, which things we should now have to get from abroad if we were to have them at all.

So general became the decay of learning in England that there were few . . . who could understand the rituals [church services] in English [Saxon], or translate a letter from Latin into English. . . . Thanks be . . . that we now have some teachers among us. . . . Consider what punishments would come upon us if we neither loved wisdom ourselves nor allowed other men to obtain it. . . .

When I thought of all this I remembered also how I saw the country before it had all been ravaged and burned; how churches throughout . . . England stood filled with treasures and books. There was also a great multitude of God's servants, but they had little knowledge of books, for they could not understand anything in them because [the books] were not written in their own language. . . .

Therefore it seems better to me . . . to translate some of the books which are most needful for all men. . . . All freeborn youth now in England, who are rich enough to devote themselves to it, [should] be set to learn as long as they are not fit for any other occupation, until they are well able to read English writing. And let those afterwards be taught more in the Latin language who are to continue learning."

vernacular tongues [native languages], he arranged to have certain basic books rendered into English [translated into Saxon].[90]

The Danes, who converted to Christianity as part of their deal with Alfred, did not entirely keep within the Danelaw, and periodic fights broke out between them and the Saxons. At the beginning of the eleventh century, the Scandinavians managed to get one of their own, Canute, on the Wessex throne. Canute was actually a legitimate heir through marriage, although

In the late 800s the Vikings began to strike against the Franks. Here, a huge fleet of Viking ships sails up the Seine River to attack Paris.

he had to kill the then Saxon king for the throne. He ruled over a superstate composed of Britain, Denmark, and Norway. This superstate, however, lasted only a few years, for upon Canute's death the Wessex throne went to another Saxon.

Vikings and Normans

In 841, some fifty years after their raids on Britain started, the Vikings began striking hard at the western Franks. In 885 a huge fleet of seven hundred Viking ships sailed up the Seine River and attacked Paris. When they could not take the city outright, the Norse set up a siege that lasted two years and ended only after the Frank-

ish emperor of the time, Charles the Fat, paid them a large sum of money and allowed them to plunder part of the western Frankish kingdom.

As they had in Britain, the Vikings built permanent bases, this time on the western coast of Europe. Most of these settlements, mainly founded by Norwegians, were located in the northwestern Frankish kingdom. The Franks began calling these Norwegian Vikings Normans, and the Norman-occupied region became known as Normandy.

In 911, the western Frankish king, Charles the Simple, made a deal with the Viking chief Rollo. If Rollo and the other Normans would stop raiding and convert to Christianity, Charles would make Rollo the duke of Normandy. Rollo accepted the offer, and one of the great powers of the Late Middle Ages was born, the duchy of Normandy. The Normans would go on to conquer England and form Norman states in Sicily, southern Italy, and the Near East.

The Rus and Kiev

In the sixth and seventh centuries, Swedish Vikings began to raid and then

---

The Vikings' Siege of Paris

In the "Wars of Count Odo with the Northmen in the Reign of Charles the Fat," *quoted in* A Source Book Of Medieval History, *The Frankish monk Abbo describes the massive effort by the Vikings to take Paris in 885-886. The defenders, led by Count Odo, managed to hold off the Vikings until the Frankish emperor Charles the Fat worked out a deal with the invaders.*

"The Northmen came to Paris with 700 sailing ships . . . [and] approached the tower [protecting the city] and attacked it. They shook it with their [war] engines and stormed it with arrows. The city resounded with clamor, the people were aroused. . . . All came together to defend the tower. . . . There perished many a Frank. . . . At last the enemy withdrew. . . . The tower had been sorely tried, but its foundations were still solid. . . . The people spent the night repairing it with boards. . . . On the old citadel [tower] had been erected a new tower of wood, a half higher than the former one. . . . Once more the [Vikings] . . . engaged with Christians in violent combat. On every side arrows sped and blood flowed. With the arrows mingled the stones hurled by slings and war-machines. . . . The tower . . . groaned with the struggle, the people ran hither and thither, the bells jangled. The warriors rushed together to defend the tottering tower. . . . Among these warriors . . . , a count . . . , surpassed all the rest in courage. . . . [This count was] Odo who never experienced defeat and continually revived the spirits of the worn-out defenders. He ran along the ramparts [defenses] and hurled back the enemy. . . .

Meanwhile Paris was suffering not only from the sword outside but also from a pestilence [disease] within. . . . Within the walls, there was not ground enough . . . to bury the dead. . . .

Now came the emperor Charles [the Fat]. . . . He allowed the Northmen to have the country of Sens [on the Yonne River] to plunder, and . . . he gave them 700 pounds of silver on condition that . . . they leave France."

---

settle along the northeastern Baltic coast. At the end of the eighth century, bands of Vikings began making long raiding expeditions into the south. Eventually the raiders set up forts along their route to protect themselves from the local inhabitants, such as the Slavs. The largest of these forts was Novgorod, which means "new fort". The Vikings finally reached and took over Kiev, where they became known as the Rus (Finnish for "Swede"), from which comes the name Russia.

In the ninth century the Slavs drove the Rus back to the Baltic. However, they soon fell to fighting among themselves, and in the 850s, according to the *Russian Primary Chronicle*, the Slavs decided to call the Rus back because

there was no law amongst them [the Slavs], but tribe rose against tribe. Discord thus ensued among them, and they began to war against one another. They said to themselves "Let us seek a prince who may rule over us . . . ac-

The Vikings invade England in 933. Becoming ever more powerful, the Vikings were able to conquer all of England.

cording to the law." They accordingly went overseas to the Varangian Russes [Swedes] . . . and said to the people of Rus, "Our whole land is great and rich, but there is no order in it. Come to rule and reign over us."[91]

A Danish Viking named Rurik used this plea as an excuse to take over Novgorod. Rurik's successor, Oleg, expanded the Rus holdings to once again include Kiev.

In 907 Oleg, with two thousand ships and eighty thousand men, attacked Constantinople and posed such a threat to the city that the Byzantine emperor agreed to a trade treaty with the Rus on Oleg's terms. This treaty turned Kiev into one of the major trade centers in Europe during the last years of the Early Middle Ages and the first of the Late. With a route that stretched from Constantinople to the east Frankish kingdom in the west and Scandinavia in the north, the Rus of Kiev linked eastern and western Europe. From the east came jewelry, silk, furs, spices, silver, and slaves, and in return from the west, wine, wheat, wool clothing, swords, and metal tools.

Viking Explorers

The Vikings were excellent shipbuilders, whose ships were far more advanced than any others to be found in the Early Middle Ages or even at the height of the Roman Empire. Their seventh-century invention of the keel gave them ships that could handle even the rough waters of the North Atlantic.

In specially designed oceangoing vessels, Viking explorers discovered Iceland in 825, settling it fifty years later. Other Norse ships would move west beyond Iceland, discovering and settling Greenland in 985 and the North American Atlantic coast in 992, which the Vikings called Vinland. Unlike the Icelandic colony, however, these other settlements would die out and be forgotten.

In the tenth century Iceland saw a surge in population as thousands of settlers came. These colonists were escaping the growing authority of the Norwegian king. Although Iceland had its own legislature, the Althing, which was established in 930 and was one of the earliest forms of representative government in the West, the island had no ruler. Powerful aristocratic families controlled Iceland, each one running its holdings as though it were an independent state. As a consequence of this lack of central authority, nothing existed to stop the many deadly feuds that broke out between upper-class Icelandic families, as David Nicholas observes: "Iceland was an exceptionally violent place, where the blood feud lived on. The freedom enjoyed by the population testifies . . . to the unwillingness of anyone to accept subordination to [the authority of] the community."[92]

Despite becoming Christians in the year 1000, Icelanders, who were of pure Viking heritage, saved and wrote down the tales and stories of the old German religion in such works as the *Elder Edda* and the *Volsunga Saga*. These Icelandic sagas, however, were more than just fiction. Some of them were records of the history of the Vikings and of Iceland. Writes Nicholas: "The atmosphere of Iceland is recreated with brutal realism in the Old Norse epics, most of which were written in Iceland."[93] The most famous of the Icelandic writers was Snorri Sturluson, who died in 1241 during one of

The Vikings were not only raiders, but explorers. One of the most well-known, Leif Ericsson, sailed to North America.

the seemingly endless Icelandic feuds. Icelandic sagas would give rise to the Late Middle Ages German epic *Nibelungenlied*, which along with the Norse originals would be used by Richard Wagner to compose his nineteenth-century opera cycle, *The Ring of the Nibelung*.

The End of the Vikings

At the end of the tenth century, which also marks the end of the Early Middle Ages, the Viking attacks stopped. In part the end came because of changes in Scandinavia. The kingdoms of Denmark, Norway, and Sweden were established, and Norse aristocrats, instead of going raiding, turned their talents to running these new realms. Further, Christianity spread through Scandinavia and replaced the old

Norse religion. The new religion, unlike the old, did not promote the warrior values of the Vikings, which died out.

In part, however, the end arrived for the Vikings when they became permanent inhabitants of Britain, Normandy, Russia, and other parts of Europe. Often, in settling down, they and their culture disappeared into that of the surrounding society. Thus, the Danes became Saxon and the Normans became Franks.

By the final years of the Early Middle Ages, the Viking period was over, and Europe—particularly western Europe—was finally free of the threat of outside invasion for the first time in five centuries. With the end of this threat, the Western world would be able to develop the civilization of the Late Middle Ages. One of the major forces in that development would be the Normans, descendants of Rollo and his Viking warriors.

The End of the Early Middle Ages

As Europe approached A.D. 1000, it was on the verge of the Late Middle Ages. However, the Early Middle Ages' effect on European development was far from over. What had happened over the past five centuries and what would happen before the beginning of the eleventh century would be important, for even as the Viking raids slowed and stopped, other events in tenth-century Europe were playing themselves out. The outcome of these events would in part govern the course that medieval civilization would take during the Late Middle Ages. In the west, new ruling families came to power to replace the now unfit Carolingians, and in the east, internal weaknesses and power struggles undercut the strength of the Byzantine and Arab empires.

The Last Carolingian Emperors

Through a series of accidents that left him emperor, as well as king of both the eastern and western Franks, Charles the Fat, the great-grandson of Charlemagne, found himself ruling over a reunited Frankish empire. However, it was a short-lived union, which was destroyed by the 885 Viking siege of Paris. Charles did almost

Charles the Fat, the great-grandson of Charlemagne, unfortunately did not live up to his esteemed heritage. He did little to repel the Viking invasions of the Frankish empire, except to bribe the Vikings to leave the kingdom alone.

nothing to help the city for two years, and when he finally made a move, it was merely to buy off the Vikings, much to the disgust of the western Franks. Within the year Charles was deposed as emperor and king of the western and eastern Franks and died soon after.

Charlemagne's imperial title lasted another twenty years, although only two emperors served during that time, one for less than a year. In 924, the last Carolingian emperor, Berengar I, was killed by his own soldiers, and the Frankish empire was dead forever.

After the Carolingians

Other Carolingians fared little better than these final emperors. In the eastern Frankish kingdom the last Carolingian king, Louis the Child, died in 911. Even before Louis's death the Carolingian rulers had lost almost all control of the kingdom to their dukes; and the duchies, such as Saxony and Bavaria, had become almost independent states. When Louis died, the dukes elected one of their own as king rather than the western Carolingian ruler, Charles the Simple.

In 919 Henry, duke of Saxony, became king of the eastern Franks and began undercutting his fellow dukes' power. His policies were continued by his son, Otto I, who took the throne in 936 and who took firm action to strengthen his hold over the eastern Franks. Historian Archibald R. Lewis writes:

> [Otto] broke the power of the independent dukes of [the] south. . . . Unlike his father, Otto relied on the Church, whose support was more de-

pendable than that of the turbulent nobility. Like the Carolingians . . . , he gave much land to bishops and abbots. In return, he required them to raise from their estates armies that would follow him into battle and to serve as administrators in his government.[94]

Otto realigned the eastern Franks with the church, giving the church land in exchange for support of his empire. Otto declared himself emperor over both the eastern Frankish kingdom (Germany) and Italy.

When the last of the Western Carolingian kings died, Hugh Capet, a Frank, was elected king.

Otto also stopped the expansion of the Magyars, who were related to the Huns and who had carved out an empire centered in Hungary.

By 962 Otto was strong enough to declare himself emperor over both the eastern Frankish kingdom, now known as Germany, and Italy, the two states together becoming the Holy Roman Empire. Otto's empire would last, at least in name, until the nineteenth century and would destroy any possibility of the unification of Germany and Italy during the Late Middle Ages. (Indeed, neither region would become a nation until the late 1800s.) Later emperors would become so involved in trying to keep the Holy Roman Empire alive that they would lose control of the individual states in both Germany and Italy. These states would function as though they were independent nations. The emperor became a figurehead, and the empire, a state without substance.

The Carolingians lasted longest in the western Frankish kingdom. The final Carolingian emperor, Louis V, died in 987 in a hunting accident. The new king, Hugh Capet, was chosen by the powerful French nobility because he was so much weaker than other French lords and thus posed no threat to them. However, Hugh, whose holding was a small region in the northern part of the kingdom that included the city of Paris, founded a line of kings who, in the Late Middle Ages, would take the western Franks from a feudal state to a nation. That nation was France.

Popes in Disgrace

As Charlemagne had been crowned emperor by the pope, so was Otto I. However, the papacy with which Otto dealt had reached an all-time low, with candidates for pope bribing, blackmailing, torturing, and killing their way into office, and with high church posts routinely being sold to the highest bidder.

At first, in the years after Charlemagne when the Carolingians rapidly lost power, the popes benefited from the decline of Carolingian influence, becoming increasingly independent of secular rulers. However, this independence was brief since, without the protection of the Frankish emperors, the popes were at the mercy of local Roman nobles. In the eight years between 896 and 904, there were "eight

Hugh Capet is crowned King of France by Archbishop Adalbert. Capet was chosen by the French nobility because he posed no threat to them.

cause the western church was now ready for "a great revival . . . [that] was to prepare the way for medieval Roman Christendom."[96] The first sign of this revival came in the tenth century when the western church converted the Slavs of central Europe and the Norse in Scandinavia.

The Byzantines

In the east the Byzantine Empire was still strong, but signs of trouble were present. The large landowners, despite imperial attempts to check their ambitions, had become more powerful, partially because they had been able to gain control of much of the imperial army. Byzantine emperors had to put down a number of revolts by these landlords and their now large private armies. The conflict between the two parties would cost the empire dearly in the first centuries of the Late Middle Ages, because having been weakened by the struggle the Byzantines lost holdings in southern Italy to the Normans and all of Asia Minor to the Seljuk Turks, who gained control of much of the Muslim world in the eleventh century.

The Byzantines also faced a growing problem in their relationship with eastern Italian cities, such as Venice. By 1000 Venice, which still looked to the Byzantine navy for protection from Muslim pirates, traded with many of the empire's eastern and western enemies. More importantly, the empire had given over management of its trade with western Europe to Venice and other Italian cities. During much of the Late Middle Ages, the Byzantines would find themselves increasingly at the mercy of Venice and other western pow-

popes in rapid succession, and the papacy . . . amid the violence and ambitions of warring nobles in Rome . . . became a pawn in the hands of a great family [that of the Roman senator Theophylactus]."[95] During the tenth century only John X emerged as a strong pope. In 916 John personally led the army that pushed the Muslims out of Italy.

As the Early Middle Ages drew to a close, the papacy continued to be a post for which candidates lied, cheated, and murdered, and church offices continued to be sold. These abuses would lead to strong reforms in the eleventh century be-ers, while threatened with extinction by hostile Muslim states.

The Muslim World

In the tenth-century Muslim world, the caliphs of Baghdad were in decline and would soon be overthrown by the Seljuk Turks, who, although Muslims, would go on to conquer the Arabs in the Near East, thus ending the Arabian empire that had flourished since the seventh century. Conflict between the Turks and the Byzantine Empire and the fear among western Christians that pilgrimages to Jerusalem would become impossible because of these new Muslim rulers led to the Christian Crusades of the Late Middle Ages.

In northern Spain small Christian kingdoms had grown up in the centuries since the Muslim conquest. These kingdoms, Navarre, Castile, and León, were weak, but in the Late Middle Ages they would take advantage of Muslim civil wars in the south to begin retaking the Spanish peninsula. This was a task that they would not finish until the middle of the fifteenth century.

So, it was now time for the Late Middle Ages. France, Germany, Constantinople, Spain, and all the rest of Europe were a stage set for this next act in the drama. Europe had its new civilization, which was no longer centered on the Mediterranean and which had been created by the five centuries of the Early Middle Ages. Historian Lewis sums up the situation:

> The eleventh century dawned on a new European civilization. . . . This new Europe was a blend of diverse traditions, peoples, and cultures. . . . This new Europe . . . was no sudden affair, but a slow process, covering a number of centuries, in which each . . . Barbarian, Merovingian, Carolingian, Viking . . . played a . . . role. . . . The story of Europe during this period [the Early Middle Ages] is not one of a dark age followed by a sudden recovery, but of a developing civilization.[97]

Notes

Introduction: A Crucial Time

1. Joseph R. Strayer, *Western Europe in the Middle Ages: A Short History*, 2nd ed. Englewood Cliffs, NJ: Prentice Hall, 1974.

2. David Nicholas, *The Evolution of the Medieval World: Society, Government, and Thought in Europe, 312-1500*. London: Longman Group, 1992.

3. Strayer, *Western Europe in the Middle Ages*.

4. Strayer, *Western Europe in the Middle Ages*.

5. James Westfall Thompson, *The Middle Ages, 300-1500*. New York: Cooper Square Publishers, 1972.

6. M. Paul Viollet, *Institutions Politiques de la France*. Translated and quoted in Thompson, *The Middle Ages*.

7. Strayer, *Western Europe in the Middle Ages*.

8. Archibald R. Lewis, *Emerging Medieval Europe, A.D. 400-1000*. New York: Knopf, 1967.

9. Justine Davis Randers-Pehrson, *Barbarians and Romans: The Birth Struggle of Europe, A.D. 400-700*. Norman: University of Oklahoma Press, 1983.

10. Norman F. Cantor, *Medieval History: The Life and Death of a Civilization*, 2nd ed. London: The Macmillan Company, 1963.

Chapter 1: The Barbarian Invasions and the Fall of Rome

11. Nicholas, *The Evolution of the Medieval World*.

12. F.W. Walbank, *The Awful Revolution: The Decline of the Roman Empire in the West*. Toronto: University of Toronto Press, 1969.

13. Tacitus, *Germania*. Edited by A.C. Howland. Quoted in Jonathan F. Scott et al., eds., *Readings in Medieval History*. New York: F.S. Crofts, 1933.

14. Tacitus, *Germania*. Quoted in Scott, *Readings in Medieval History*.

15. Crane Brinton et al., *A History of Civilization*, vol. 1, *Prehistory to 1715*, 2nd ed. Englewood Cliffs, NJ: Prentice Hall, 1960.

16. Jordanes, *Gothic History*. Quoted in Will Durant, *The Story of Civilization*, vol. 4, *The Age of Faith*. New York: Simon and Schuster, 1950.

17. Theodoric the Great, *The Letters of Cassiodorus*. Translated by Thomas Hodgkin. Quoted in Brian Tierney, ed., *The Middle Ages*, vol. 1, *Sources of Medieval History*, 3rd ed. New York: Knopf, 1978.

18. Procopius, *History of the Wars*. Quoted in Durant, *The Story of Civilization*.

19. Nicholas, *The Evolution of the Medieval World*.

Chapter 2: Upon This Rock: The Importance of the Christian Church

20. Brinton, *A History of Civilization*.

21. David Knowles and Dimitri Obolensky, *The Christian Centuries*, vol. 2, *The Middle Ages*. New York: McGraw-Hill, 1968.

22. Brinton, *A History of Civilization*.

23. Nicholas, *The Evolution of the Medieval World*.

24. Durant, *The Story of Civilization*.

25. Norman F. Cantor, *The Civilization of the Middle Ages*. New York: HarperCollins, 1993.

26. Pope Gregory I, *Library of Nicene and Post-Nicene Fathers*. Translated by James Barmby. Quoted in C. Warren Hollister et al., *Medieval Europe: A Short Sourcebook*. New York: John Wiley, 1982.

27. Nicholas, *The Evolution of the Medieval World*.

28. Saint Benedict, *The Rule of St. Benedict.* Translated by Marc Anthony Meyer. Quoted in Hollister, *Medieval Europe.*

29. Brinton, *A History of Civilization.*

30. Saint Benedict. Quoted in Durant, *The Story of Civilization.*

31. Knowles and Obolensky, *The Christian Centuries.*

32. Nicholas, *The Evolution of the Medieval World.*

Chapter 3: Kingdom and Empire in the West: The Franks

33. Gregory of Tours, *History of the Franks.* Edited by O.M. Dalton. Quoted in Brinton, *A History of Civilization.*

34. Einhard, *The Emperor Karl the Great [Charlemagne].* Translated by William Glaister. Quoted in Scott, *Readings in Medieval History.*

35. Louis the Pious, *Ordinatio Imperii.* Quoted in Brian Pullan, *Sources for the History of Medieval Europe, from the Mid-Eighth to the Mid-Thirteenth Century,* corrected ed. Oxford: Basil Blackwell, 1971.

36. Brinton, *A History of Civilization.*

37. Cantor, *The Civilization of the Middle Ages.*

38. Cantor, *The Civilization of the Middle Ages.*

39. Nicholas, *The Evolution of the Medieval World.*

40. Durant, *The Story of Civilization.*

41. Einhard, *Early Lives of Charlemagne.* Edited by A.J. Grant. Quoted in Brinton, *A History of Civilization.*

42. Nicholas, *The Evolution of the Medieval World.*

Chapter 4: The New Social Order: The Growth of Feudalism

43. Brinton, *A History of Civilization.*

44. George B. Adams, *Civilization During the Middle Ages.* Quoted in Scott, *Readings in Medieval History.*

45. "Frankish Commendation." Translated and edited by E.P. Cheyney. Quoted in Hollister, *Medieval Europe.*

46. F.L. Ganshof, *Feudalism.* Translated by Philip Grierson. New York: Harper Torchbooks, 1952.

47. Durant, *The Story of Civilization.*

48. Dhuoda, wife of the Marquis Bernard de Septimania. Quoted in Ganshof, *Feudalism.*

49. "Bureau of Treasury Accounts." Translated by Edward P. Cheyney. Quoted in Frederic Austin Ogg, ed., *A Source Book of Medieval History.* New York: Cooper Square Publishers, 1907.

50. Ganshof, *Feudalism.*

51. Nicholas, *The Evolution of the Medieval World.*

52. The Right Honorable Lord Ernle (Rowland E. Prothero), *English Farming, Past and Present.* Quoted in Scott, *Readings in Medieval History.*

53. Nicholas, *The Evolution of the Medieval World.*

54. Brinton, *A History of Civilization.*

55. Durant, *The Story of Civilization.*

56. Nicholas, *The Evolution of the Medieval World.*

57. Cantor, *The Civilization of the Middle Ages.*

Chapter 5: Empire in the East: The Byzantines

58. Nicholas, *The Evolution of the Medieval World.*

59. Brinton, *A History of Civilization.*

60. Nicholas, *The Evolution of the Medieval World.*

61. Nicholas, *The Evolution of the Medieval World.*

62. Brinton, *A History of Civilization.*

63. Procopius. Quoted in Brinton, *A History of Civilization.*

64. Durant, *The Story of Civilization.*

65. Procopius, *Secret History.* Translated by H.B. Dewing. Quoted in Durant, *The Story of Civilization.*

66. *The Civil Law.* Translated by S.P. Scott. Quoted in Charles T. Davis, ed., *The Eagle, the Crescent, and the Cross: Sources of Medieval History,* vol. 1 (ca. 250-ca.1000). New York: Appleton-Century-Crofts, 1967.

67. Cantor, *The Civilization of the Middle Ages.*

68. Durant, *The Story of Civilization.*

69. Procopius, *History of the Wars.* Quoted in Brinton, *A History of Civilization.*

70. A.P. Vlasto, *The Entry of the Slavs into Christendom: An Introduction to the Medieval History of the Slavs.* Cambridge, England: Cambridge University Press, 1970.

71. Durant, *The Story of Civilization.*

72. Harry J. Magoulias, *Byzantine Christianity: Emperor, Church, and the West.* Detroit: Wayne State University Press, 1970.

73. Durant, *The Story of Civilization.*

Chapter 6: The New Religion: Islam and Southern Europe

74. Muhammad. Quoted in Durant, *The Story of Civilization.*

75. Durant, *The Story of Civilization.*

76. Cantor, *The Civilization of the Middle Ages.*

77. Cantor, *The Civilization of the Middle Ages.*

78. Philip K. Hitti, *The Arabs: A Short History.* Quoted in Nicholas, *The Evolution of the Medieval World.*

79. Brinton, *A History of Civilization.*

80. Muhammad. Quoted in Durant, *The Story of Civilization.*

81. Durant, *The Story of Civilization.*

82. J.W. Draper, *History of the Intellectual Development of Europe.* Quoted in Scott, *Readings in Medieval History.*

83. Quoted in Brinton, *A History of Civilization.*

Chapter 7: The Last of the Barbarians: The Vikings

84. Brinton, *A History of Civilization.*

85. Durant, *The Story of Civilization.*

86. Ibn Fadlan. Translated by E. Bannister-Good. Quoted in Davis, *The Eagle, the Crescent, and the Cross.*

87. Nicholas, *The Evolution of the Medieval World.*

88. *Annals of Xanten.* Translated by James H. Robinson. Quoted in Ogg, *A Source Book of Medieval History.*

89. *Anglo-Saxon Chronicle.* Translated by Ingram. Quoted in Durant, *The Story of Civilization.*

90. Durant, *The Story of Civilization.*

91. *Russian Primary Chronicle.* Translated and edited by Samuel H. Cross, quoted in Brinton, *A History of Civilization.*

92. Nicholas, *The Evolution of the Medieval World.*

93. Nicholas, *The Evolution of the Medieval World.*

Epilogue: The End of the Early Middle Ages

94. Lewis, *Emerging Medieval Europe.*

95. Knowles and Obolensky, *The Christian Centuries.*

96. Brinton, *A History of Civilization.*

97. Lewis, *Emerging Medieval Europe.*

Glossary

abbot: The head of a monastery.

Arianism: An early brand of Christianity that did not accept God, Christ, and the Holy Ghost as equal parts of a single being, the Trinity.

barbarian: To the Romans, any group of people who did not speak Latin or Greek.

Benedictines: Members of a monastic order, founded by Saint Benedict in 529, who set up hospitals, orphanages, and schools during the Early Middle Ages.

benefice: A feudal grant, also called a fief, presented to a vassal, which often gave him control of a manor.

bishop: A church official who supervised several churches in an administrative region called a bishopric or see.

Byzantine Empire: The eastern half of the Roman Empire that survived throughout the Middle Ages and whose capital was Constantinople or Byzantium (today Istanbul).

Carolingians: The Frankish line of kings and emperors to whom Charlemagne belonged.

fealty: An oath of loyalty given by a vassal to a lord, often in exchange for a benefice, or fief.

feudalism: The political, social, and economic system under which much of medieval Europe operated. It involved oaths of fealty between the nobility that pledged service, particularly military, in exchange for benefices, or fiefs.

fief: A feudal grant, also called a benefice, presented to a vassal, which often gave him control of a manor.

Franks: German tribe who conquered most of western Europe, out of whose territory eventually came France and Germany.

Gaul: Part of the western Roman Empire that covered most of what is now France.

Goths: German barbarians who settled in what is now Romania, who were divided into two groups, the Visigoths and Ostrogoths, and who eventually invaded the Roman Empire.

hierarchy: The ordered ranking of officials in an organization or system.

Iconoclasm: The practice of destroying religious images; the name of an eighth-century Byzantine religious movement that claimed that the worship of holy statues and images was sinful.

Islam: The religion founded by the Arabian prophet Muhammad.

jihad: A holy struggle, often a war, that spreads the principles of Islam through the seizure of political power.

knight: Horse-mounted armored warrior. Knights were generally recruited from the nobility.

Koran: The holy book of Islam that contains the teachings of Muhammad.

Lombards: German tribe that established a kingdom in northern Italy in the sixth century.

lord: A noble, also known as a suzerain, to whom a vassal gave an oath of fealty.

manor: A medieval farming estate that was virtually a self-contained community. The control of such an estate was given as a fief to a vassal.

march: A frontier province of the Frankish kingdom.

medieval: Refers to anyone or anything associated with the Middle Ages.

Merovingians: The line of kings founded by the Frankish chieftain Clovis.

monasticism: A church movement in which the practitioners, known as monks, lived in isolated communities, monasteries, in order to get closer to God. The monks considered self-denial and charity important in achieving their goal.

Muslim: A follower of Islam.

Norse: German tribes living in Scandinavia, whose sea-roving raiders, the Vikings, terrorized Europe in the ninth and tenth centuries.

Ostrogoths: The eastern Goths, who under Theodoric the Great formed a kingdom in Italy at the end of the fifth century.

papacy: The office of the pope.

renaissance: A rebirth; generally refers to a reawakening of art and learning. When capitalized, it refers to the period in European history following the Middle Ages.

Saxons: German tribe, part of whom, along with the Angles and the Jutes, overran the island of Britain beginning in the fifth century. The remainder of the tribe was conquered by Charlemagne at the end of the eighth century.

secular: Refers to anything not a part of the church, such as civil government.

serf: Worker on a manor whose position was hereditary and who could not leave the manor without the landlord's permission.

suzerain: A noble, also known as a lord, to whom a vassal gave an oath of fealty.

vassal: A noble who pledged his fealty to another noble, known as a lord or suzerain.

Vikings: Sea-roving Norse raiders from Scandinavia who terrorized Europe during the ninth and tenth centuries.

Visigoths: The western Goths, who founded a kingdom in Spain that was ended by the Muslims in the eighth century.

For Further Reading

Isaac Asimov, *The Dark Ages*. Boston: Houghton Mifflin, 1968. A thorough, detailed retelling of the events that shaped the Early Middle Ages. This book has a number of useful maps showing Europe at various times during the period, as well as charts showing the relationships of the various Merovingian and Carolingian kings.

Thomas Bulfinch, *Legends of Charlemagne* in *Bulfinch's Mythology*. New York: Thomas Y. Crowell, 1970. A lively and readable retelling of the fictitious medieval stories about Charlemagne and his paladins. The introduction gives useful information about the background of the tales.

Giovanni Caselli, *A Medieval Monk*. New York: Bedrick, 1986. A good account of a year in the life of a young Benedictine monk. Well illustrated by the author; includes a glossary and selected bibliography.

———, *A Viking Settler*. New York: Bedrick, 1986. Filled with interesting details about day-to-day life on a farm in tenth-century Denmark. Good illustrations by the author, along with a glossary and selected bibliography, accompany the text.

Ives Cohat, *The Vikings: Lords of the Sea*. Translated by Ruth Daniel. New York: Harry N. Abrams, 1992. A short history of the Vikings—who they were and what they did. Lavishly illustrated, with many plates in color.

Aryeh Grabois, *Illustrated Encyclopedia of Medieval Civilization*. New York: Octopus, 1980. Several hundred entries provide good, detailed information on medieval terms, people, and events. Excellent photographs, many of them full page and in color, enrich the text, as do the very useful map section, time line, and bibliography.

Susan Howarth, *Medieval People*. Brookfield, CT: Millbrook Press, 1992. A good source for learning about various medieval occupations, such as king, nun, doctor, and pope. Plenty of information, some of it from firsthand accounts, is enhanced by color illustrations, a glossary, and a bibliography.

———, *Medieval Places*. Brookfield, CT: Millbrook Press, 1992. Useful and detailed look at such parts of medieval life as a village, a battlefield, and a parish church. Text supported by illustrations, some in color, a glossary, and a bibliography.

Donald Matthew, *Atlas of Medieval Europe*. New York: Facts on File, 1983. Filled with large, easily read maps in color and well-reproduced photographs, mostly in color. A good commentary with special sections on such topics as the Carolingian renaissance and the Christian church is supported by a time line and a bibliography arranged by country and topic.

Mokhtar Moktefi, *The Rise of Islam*. Englewood Cliffs, NJ: Silver Burdett, 1986. A fact-filled account of the early history of Islam that also looks at the achievements of the Muslim culture in the Early Middle Ages. Two concluding sections present Muslim fables and articles on the Arabic language. Lavishly illustrated in color.

Ewart O. Oakeshott, *Dark Age Warrior*. Chester Springs, PA: Dufour, 1984. A readable history of the German migration that also goes into tribal religion, organization, and life. Text is supported by detailed line drawings.

The Song of Roland, translated by Glynn Burgess. London: Penguin, 1990. A modern verse translation of one of the most important epic poems of the Middle Ages and the most famous of the Charlemagne legends.

Additional Works Consulted

Crane Brinton, John B. Christopher, and Robert Lee Wolff, *A History of Civilization*, vol. 1, *Prehistory to 1715*, 2nd ed. Englewood Cliffs, NJ: Prentice Hall, 1960. The chapters on the Early Middle Ages give a clear outline, as well as presenting a balanced account, of the period.

Norman F. Cantor, *The Civilization of the Middle Ages*. New York: HarperCollins, 1993. A thorough, updated history of the Middle Ages by an eminent medieval scholar. The book provides facts and insights into the people and events of the Early Middle Ages, as well as a useful reading list, and even a list of recommended films about the Middle Ages.

———, *Medieval History: The Life and Death of a Civilization*. New York: The Macmillan Company, 1963. An earlier version of *The Civilization of the Middle Ages*, containing sound information that was eliminated from the later book. This edition also has valuable listings of medieval popes and Byzantine emperors.

J.S. Critchley, *Feudalism*. London: George Allen and Unwin, 1978. Takes each part of feudalism, such as fiefs, lords, and vassals, and explains what it is and how it fitted into the feudal system.

Charles T. Davis, ed., *The Eagle, the Crescent, and the Cross: Sources of Medieval History*, vol. 1 (ca. 250-ca. 1000). New York: Appleton-Century-Crofts, 1967. An excellent source of Early Middle Ages writing. Each piece is either by or about a major figure from the period.

Will Durant, *The Story of Civilization*, vol. 4, *The Age of Faith*. New York: Simon and Schuster, 1950. A classic study of the Middle Ages that is written in a readable and accessible style and that ends with a large bibliography. Its chapters on the Early Middle Ages are filled with facts, incidents, and speculation about the time.

F.L. Ganshof, *Feudalism*. Translated by Philip Grierson. New York: Harper Torchbooks, 1952. The first part of this well-known book is a good, sound history of the development of feudalism, and the second is a description of what the feudal system was and how it operated.

Bernard Grun, *The Timetables of History: A Horizontal Linkage of People and Events*, rev. ed. Based on Werner Stein, *Kulturfahrplan*. New York: Simon and Schuster, 1979. A useful book that shows year by year, and in chart form, the important people and events, as well as landmarks in art, religion, education, science, and daily life, from earliest history to the present.

C. Warren Hollister et al., eds., *Medieval Europe: A Short Sourcebook*. New York: John Wiley, 1982. A useful, if limited, selection of original writings from the Early Middle Ages, most of which are modern translations.

David Knowles and Dimitri Obolensky, *The Christian Centuries*, vol. 2, *The Middle Ages*. New York: McGraw-Hill, 1968. A thorough and scholarly history of both the western and eastern Orthodox church in the Early Middle Ages. The book has a valuable time line of events, a listing of popes, and a large number of photographs of medieval church buildings and art.

Archibald R. Lewis, *Emerging Medieval Europe, A.D. 400-1000*. New York: Knopf, 1967. A short history of the Early Middle Ages that looks at both western and eastern Europe and that emphasizes the social changes of the period.

Harry J. Magoulias, *Byzantine Christianity: Emperor, Church, and the West*. Detroit: Wayne State University Press, 1970. A scholarly study of the nature of the Eastern Orthodox Church and its importance to the development and political aims of the Byzantine empire.

David Nicholas, *The Evolution of the Medieval World: Society, Government, and Thought in Europe, 312-1500*. London: Longman Group, 1992. A revisionist look at the history of the Middle Ages that shows how religion, politics, art, and everyday life contributed to the evolutionary development of the period from the fall of Rome to the Renaissance. Each chapter ends with a list of suggested readings, and the book has an excellent map section at the back.

Frederic Austin Ogg, ed., *A Source Book of Medieval History*. New York: Cooper Square Publishers, 1907. One of the best sources for original writings from the Early Middle Ages. Lengthy excerpts from period documents have thoughtful introductions that explain the importance of each selection.

Brian Pullan, *Sources for the History of Medieval Europe, from the Mid-Eighth to the Mid-Thirteenth Century*, corrected ed. Oxford: Basil Blackwell, 1971. A large selection of original Early Middle Ages writings, newly translated for this book, about the papacy, feudalism, and Islam.

Justine Davis Randers-Pehrson, *Barbarians and Romans: The Birth Struggle of Europe, A.D. 400-700*. Norman: University of Oklahoma Press, 1983. An extensive look at the major German tribes and the kingdoms each established at the beginning of the Early Middle Ages. The book has many excellent photographs of German artifacts, a number in color.

Jonathan F. Scott, Albert Hyma, and Arthur H. Noyes, eds., *Readings in Medieval History*. New York: F.S. Crofts, 1933. A classic source of original writings from the Early Middle Ages, particularly useful for material about the medieval Catholic Church and feudalism.

Joseph R. Strayer, *Western Europe in the Middle Ages: A Short History*, 2nd ed. Englewood Cliffs, NJ: Prentice Hall, 1974. The first two parts of this book by a famous medieval scholar constitute a good, short history of the Early Middle Ages, with particular emphasis on Charlemagne and the Carolingian empire.

James Westfall Thompson, *The Middle Ages, 300-1500*. New York: Cooper Square Publishers, 1972. A scholarly and revisionist history of the Middle Ages.

Brian Tierney, ed., *The Middle Ages*, vol. 1, *Sources of Medieval History*, 3rd ed. New York: Knopf, 1978. A useful, short collection of original writings from the Early Middle Ages.

Malcolm Todd, *Everyday Life of the Barbarians: Goths, Franks, and Vandals*. New York: G.P. Putnam's Sons, 1972. A detailed study of the German tribes that presents their social structure, everyday life, religion, art, and warfare. This book is filled with drawings and photographs of German artifacts.

A.P. Vlasto, *The Entry of the Slavs into Christendom: An Introduction to the Medieval History of the Slavs*. Cambridge, England: Cambridge University Press, 1970. A scholarly history of the migration of the Slavs into eastern Europe and of the kingdoms they founded.

F.W. Walbank, *The Awful Revolution: The Decline of the Roman Empire in the West*. Toronto: University of Toronto Press, 1969. A general history of the last centuries of the western Roman Empire and the beginnings of the Early Middle Ages.

Index

Picture Credits

About the Author

James A. Corrick has been a professional writer and editor for more than fifteen years and is the author of a dozen books, as well as close to two hundred articles and short stories. His most recent books are *Mars, Muscular Dystrophy, Human Genetic Engineering*, and another Lucent Book, *The Late Middle Ages*. Along with having a doctorate in English, Corrick's diverse academic background includes a graduate degree in the biological sciences. He has taught English, tutored minority students, edited three different magazines for the National Space Society, and been a science writer for the Muscular Dystrophy Association. He lives in Tucson, Arizona, with a constantly changing number of dogs, cats, and books. When not writing, Corrick reads, swims, lifts weights, takes long walks, frequents bookstores, and holds forth on any number of topics. Currently he is the secretary of the Tucson Book Publishing Association and a member of the Arizona Historical Society.